HERE

and

QUEER

Rowan Ellis   **Jacky Sheridan**

Rowan Ellis is a writer, video essayist and LGBTQI+ advocate based in the UK who creates content around queer history, pop culture and activism. Her work has been covered in publications including Forbes, The Guardian, Teen Vogue, Elle UK and BBC. She is also the co-founder and co-organiser of Ruckus Retreat, a residential retreat for creatives. She lives in London with her two cats – Persephone and Ichabod – and an oven perpetually full of baked goods.

Jacky Sheridan is a bisexual Irish illustrator who uses her unique humour and a high contrast illustrative style to create expressive, fun, bold and engaging work. She also often lends her illustration talent to artistic activism around causes close to her heart such as queer rights and sexuality, feminism, reproductive rights and body positivity.

Instagram: @jackysheridan
Website: http://www.jackysheridan.com/

Photograph by Billy Woods

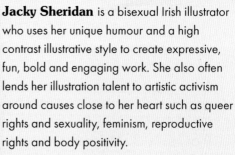

Hafsa Qureshi is an openly bisexual Muslim activist. She works to raise visibility and build awareness of queer Muslims just like her.

Mikaela Moody is a white, disfigured, non-binary lesbian trans woman living in the Midlands, UK. When not wishing she was back in Florida with her girlfriend and close friends, Mikaela writes (and listens to) music, plays a bunch of different video games, alternates between doing activism and really needing a break from it and obsesses over Muppets.

Annie Segarra, also known as Annie Elainey, is an American YouTuber, artist and activist for LGBT and disability rights. Segarra, who is queer, Latinx and disabled, advocates for accessibility, body positivity and media representation of marginalised communities.

Maz Hedgehog is a writer, editor and performer working in the spaces between real and unreal, poetry and theatre, self and other. Their work has found its way onto stages and behind mics across the UK. Fond of fairies and folklore, Maz's work is imaginative, lyrical and occasionally a little surreal. Find them across social media @MazHedgehog.

CONTENTS

PART THREE: FINDING YOUR COMMUNITY

INTRODUCTION

Hello, and welcome to this growing-up guide for queer girls – packed full of information about our culture, relationships and history.

I'm Rowan, a queer creator who makes videos about LGBTQ+ history and pop culture, and apparently now writes books about them too! This book answers questions like, 'How do I find queer friends?', 'What counts as sex with a girl?', and 'How can I celebrate Pride if I don't live near a parade?' Being queer has brought such strength, joy and friendship to my life – and I'm so excited to share it with you.

We'll look at the wonderful things about being a queer girl, but also some struggles you might be going through. I didn't want to sugarcoat or ignore experiences you might be familiar with, including homophobia and sexism. But I also didn't want to fall into that gloomy trope of queer pain and suffering being all there is to our collective story.

Each of us has our own unique experience of being queer; I knew that there would be things other queer people have gone through that I hadn't. So, I asked four of my friends, who also happen to be queer activists, artists, performers and more, to share their own experiences. It's my hope that readers of this book might either be able to learn from them, or see themselves reflected in their stories, which you'll find scattered through the book.

I feel it's important to say that this book was written with the intention of being trans-inclusive. Trans women are women, and trans girls are girls – so of course queer trans girls are welcome in the pages of this book! For example, the chapter about sex doesn't make any assumptions about your body, or the bodies of your partners' – and we talk a little about transmisogyny.

I'm also aware you might be in possession of this book now, but later realise you aren't actually a girl like people had always assumed – or maybe you have some other messy gender-y feelings that mean you are no longer a queer 'girl'. Hopefully, this book will still provide you with information on a history and culture that is interesting for anyone to read. And you can always pass the book along to a queer girl in your life for a bit of queer solidarity!

I wrote this with the knowledge that it was exactly what I needed but didn't have when I was a queer teen. I hope you were recommended this book by a woman with a rainbow pin in your local book shop when you finally felt brave enough to ask. I hope your parent or sibling or friend gifted this to you in an act of love and support after you came out to them. I hope you make eye contact with a cute girl while reading this on the train and she gives you a shy smile when she sees the front cover. More than anything, I hope this book makes you feel seen – because I see you, and you deserve it.

Rowan Ellis

CHAPTER ONE
How Do I Know I'm Gay (or Bi, or Pan or...)?

So, you've picked up this book and turned to the first chapter. You're ready for me to give you the 101 shortcut guide to definitively confirming your sexuality. I would love to say it's as easy as taking a quick online quiz (pick your ideal fast food order and we'll tell you your sexuality). But for a lot of us, IT JUST ISN'T THAT SIMPLE.

You are the only person who knows if you're gay, or bi, or pan, or ace or any other identity on the wonderful LGBTQ+ spectrum. I know reading that will fill some of you with relief; it can be affirming to hear that other people can't define who you are. But I also know some of you will be saying, 'Rowan, that's not a real answer. I legitimately need to know if I'm gay – can't you just tell me?'

The truth is that no one can decide for you.

But it doesn't mean you have to go through that journey alone. Something that can really help is talking to people who you know will be supportive – maybe a friend, sibling or counsellor. You might think that the first time you talk about your sexuality with someone else, you have to come out. But that isn't the case at all!

My first tentative conversations about sexuality were in an online forum for LGBTQ+ teenagers, and I spent a long time lurking and reading other people's posts before I ever said anything. When I finally started posting, I asked questions and talked about how I was feeling – all without labelling myself to my new friends. I even went to a few meet-ups while thinking of myself as a straight ally. I remember sitting in the sun surrounded by my new friends, some wearing rainbow pins and bright dungarees, others dressed in grungy jeans with shaggy hair. From the outside we probably looked like a grab-bag of different high school cliques – very *Breakfast Club*-chic. It was the first time I'd been asked to introduce myself with my name and pronouns. I was worried – was this a space for people who had already figured everything out? But the host of the meet-up continued, 'It's just so we know if you have a preference right now that we should use. If you aren't sure, you can always say different pronouns next time we meet'. I remember falling back onto the parched summer grass and letting the laughter and voices of my new friends wash over me like a blanket. Talking with them wrapped me up in a feeling of absolute safety – it was a space where it was okay to not be sure.

A year later I was marching with that same group at Pride. So what happened in between to get me from shyly chatting online, to openly singing chants as we danced along the parade route?

There are three things that feed into working out your sexuality. Let me explain.

1. WHAT YOU THINK AND FEEL

We'll start with your thoughts and feelings, the first aspect of this messy sexuality triangle. These can sometimes be influenced by people around you. When you look at people who are already out, you might think: **'If I'm not sure like they are, does that mean I can't really be queer? People are sure about these things, right?'** In fact, most people who are confident and proud once felt just like you – they had to figure themselves out.

Even if your friends, family and school are supportive, it can still feel scary or difficult to figure out your sexuality. One reason for that is the assumption that everyone is straight until proven otherwise. Most media you watch or read, the adverts on the TV and the songs you hear on the radio all have a focus on straight people. This is called **heteronormativity** – the idea that heterosexuality is the default in our society. This might lead you to experience what's called **compulsory heterosexuality** or **comp het** – the social pressures that tell you that you should automatically like boys if you are a girl. For some people, it can be difficult to figure out if they really like boys, or if it's just something they've been told you have to feel. Despite what heteronormativity may lead you

to believe, liking other girls is totally normal. So, an important first step is trying to put aside how other people feel and focus on yourself. How do *you* feel?

There are different ways in which you might feel attraction to others, such as physical, sexual, emotional or romantic. You might feel one, all or a mix of those things towards people of different genders. Maybe you've thought, 'Oh no, she's cute' about a friend. Or felt nervous butterflies when you look at a famous musician. Maybe you imagine holding hands with a girl, or what it would be like to kiss her. You might get turned on by women in books, TV shows, fanfic – or even scenarios in your imagination.

All of these can be indicators of attraction to girls and these alone may be enough for you to realise you aren't straight. You don't necessarily have to have done anything physical or romantic with another girl to know who you are – after all, we don't expect every straight girl to prove they're really straight! And, you might not feel sexual or romantic attraction to anyone. But if you have had that kind of experience it might help confirm how you feel. That brings us onto the second side of the triangle…

So, an important first step is trying to put aside
how other people feel and focus on yourself.

HOW DO YOU FEEL?

2. WHAT YOU DO

HEAD TO CHAPTER 10 ON PAGE 82 TO READ ABOUT CONSENT AND COMMUNICATION.

Maybe you've thought about kissing or holding hands with another girl. You might have even had romantic or sexual encounters with girls before. Doing these things doesn't automatically make you queer. Similarly, you might have dated boys before – and that doesn't make you straight. It's how you feel about them that counts. I know, I know, back to the feelings. But they really are the only way for you to figure this all out.

Once you have your feelings figured out, it's time for the final side of the triangle…

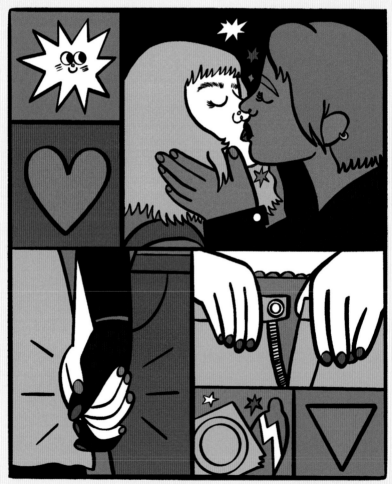

3. HOW YOU IDENTIFY

The LGBTQ+ community is sometimes described as a spectrum, but I see it more as a big map. Your coordinates on the map can be anywhere, not just a point on a line between gay and straight. Look at the definitions of different sexual orientations and see which ones match up with your feelings (don't worry, we'll go over this in the next chapter).

To help, you could check out videos, podcasts or books by people with different identities, and see what words feel right for you. Hearing other people's experiences can often resonate with our own, and help us find an identity that fits.

For example, two girls who both feel attraction to people of all genders might choose different words to describe themselves – one might go with 'pansexual', while the other might feel more into 'queer'. A third girl, who feels the same way, might decide to not use any labels at all to define her sexuality – and that's totally valid too.

It's important to know that if you land on your coordinates on the LGBTQ+ map, you don't have to stay there forever. Some people find their place on the map and make it their home. But it's just as valid to be someone who finds themselves voyaging around the map. It's okay to keep figuring things out about yourself, to change your identity or to develop feelings for people of genders you hadn't felt romantically or sexually about before.

Some of you might also be figuring things out with your gender identity. You might know you like girls, but then come to realise that you aren't a girl yourself. In that case, your feelings and thoughts about girls might stay the same, but the words you use for your identity might shift – for example, from gay girl to straight boy.

There's no need to rush. Trust yourself, reach out for support through the journey and know that

YOU ARE IN CONTROL OF YOUR OWN IDENTITY.

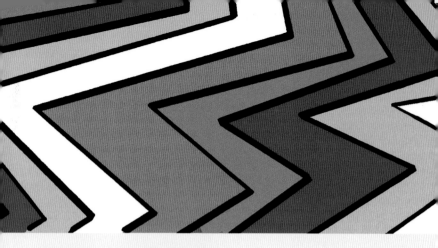

CHAPTER TWO
LGBTQ+
Identities & Terms

So, what kinds of words might you use to describe yourself? Before we take a look at different identities across the LGBTQ+ community, it's useful to note that some of these words will mean different things to different people. While writing this, I asked friends to send me their own definitions of their sexuality and gender identities – and even people who use the same word to describe themselves had slightly different ways of defining it. And that's totally okay! After all, there isn't an Official Global Queer Committee that decides what words we should use and what they should mean to everyone.

Instead, communities throughout our history found or created words they liked and began to use them. Those words were passed on verbally, through writing or people moving around and (more recently) the internet. Labels can broadly describe identities but don't necessarily need to strictly define them. And new words are still being created today when we find a gap in our language. For example, if you are non-binary and are only attracted to other non-binary people – what might you call yourself?

In the glossary below I've given one definition for each word. If a word resonates with you but its definition here doesn't quite fit how you feel, I'd recommend seeing if there are other definitions of the word that might make it fit better for you personally. It's also worth noting that this isn't an exhaustive list of every sexuality and gender identity – there may well be a word (or a few different words) not defined here that work best for you.

AGENDER
A person who feels no (or very little) connection to gender, identifies as genderless or sees themselves as gender neutral.

AROMANTIC/ARO
Someone who experiences little or no romantic attraction to other people.

ASEXUAL/ACE
Someone who experiences little or no sexual attraction to other people.

BISEXUAL/BI
Someone with the potential to be romantically and/or sexually attracted to people of more than one sex and/or gender. These attractions don't necessarily manifest in the same way, to the same degree or at the same time.

CISGENDER/CIS
A person whose gender identity matches the sex and gender they were assumed to be at birth.

CISNORMATIVITY
The assumption across society that everyone is cisgender and the only right way to identify and express your gender is through the gender binary.

DEADNAME
The name given to a transgender person at birth, which they often change

at some point during their transition and no longer use.

GAY
Refers to someone who is romantically and/or sexually attracted to people of the same gender. Historically, it was most commonly used to describe men, but is now also used by many as an umbrella term.

GENDER BINARY
The idea that people can be classified into one of just two distinct and opposite genders — male or female. The gender binary often supports the idea that people will align closely with socially constructed ideas of masculinity (if they're male) or femininity (if they're female). It is a very limited idea of gender and gender expression.

GENDER EXPRESSION
The way in which we present ourselves (including clothing, hairstyles and behaviour) which might be associated with how the world views gender. Your gender expression and gender identity don't have to 'match' — you might identify as a girl but enjoy presenting yourself in a way that society deems as 'masculine', for example.

GENDER FLUID
Someone who doesn't identify with a single fixed gender, or has a gender identity that may shift.

GENDER IDENTITY
Our personal understanding and experience of our own gender, and how we label our gender.

GENDERQUEER
Someone whose gender identity is outside of fixed labels and binaries of gender.

HETERONORMATIVITY
The assumption across society that everyone is straight and that heterosexuality is the only 'correct' sexuality.

INTERSEX
An umbrella term for people who are born with

a chromosomal pattern, reproductive system, hormone make-up and/or sexual anatomy that does not fit typical binary ideas of male or female bodies.

LGBTQ+

An umbrella term for the community. It stands for Lesbian, Gay, Bisexual, Transgender and Queer/Questioning, with the plus sign representing other sexualities and gender identities not covered by the other letters.

LESBIAN

A girl who is specifically romantically and/or sexually attracted to other girls. Some non-binary people also relate to this label.

NON-BINARY

An umbrella term for anyone with a gender identity that is not only male or only female, and this might include identifying with no gender, multiple genders or a new gender entirely. For some people, their gender identity can shift or be 'fluid' across their life or day to day.

PANSEXUAL/PAN

Someone who has the potential to be attracted to all gender identities/expressions.

PRONOUNS

A word to refer to someone you are talking about, e.g. she/her, he/him, they/them. These words often 'match up' with someone's gender, but they don't always. There are also less well-known pronouns, and people who use multiple pronouns, e.g. she/they, ze/zir.

QUEER

A word that has been used as both a slur against the community and as a reclaimed umbrella term for it. It is used as an identity label by individuals for a number of reasons including as a catch-all term when they have multiple queer identities (e.g. gay and asexual), or for people who feel like other more defined labels don't fit them.

QUESTIONING
Someone who is not sure or exploring how they identify in terms of their sexuality and/or gender identity.

SAPPHIC
An umbrella term that includes any woman who experiences any attraction to other women (including bi, lesbian, pan and queer women).

STRAIGHT/HETEROSEXUAL
Refers to someone who is romantically and/or sexually attracted only to people of the other binary (male/female) gender.

TRANSGENDER/TRANS
Sometimes used specifically to refer to someone who transitions between binary genders of male and female, but can also be used as an umbrella term for anyone whose gender identity doesn't match the sex and gender that they were assumed to be at birth.

Something really interesting about identity language is that it can change over time. Take the term 'LGBTQ+' for example. Over the years there have been lots of names used to describe this same group of people (e.g. gay community, LGBT, LGBTQIAA, QUILTBAG, queer community, etc.). But it has so many different people and identities within it, that coming up with one word or phrase that feels inclusive to everyone is trickier than it seems! There are also words like 'queer' and 'dyke', which were historically used as slurs but have been reclaimed by some people – and there will always be new slang words used across different groups.

This might feel overwhelming at first, but you can always ask what an unfamiliar word means or look it up online to find out more. And who knows, you might find a new word for something you've been struggling to articulate about yourself!

CHAPTER THREE
Coming Out

Okay, so you've thought it through and worked out how you want to identify. What happens next? Well, for a lot of us, this is the bit where we tell other people about our identity – the queer rite of passage known as 'coming out'. A question commonly asked by young queer people is: 'how do I know when I'm ready to come out?' Sadly, we are not cakes – we can't just set a timer and come out of the (metaphorical) sexuality oven perfectly cooked. Some people are ready right away, but others need more time. I know it sounds like another cop-out answer from me, but it really does vary because everyone's circumstances are different. So instead of telling you – yes, you, the person reading this right now – if you should come out, in this chapter I'm going to give you some things you might want to think about when deciding to come out.

THE GOOD THINGS ABOUT COMING OUT

First, I want to talk about some reasons why people come out. So often, conversations about coming out are filled with warnings and dread – but it can also be a moment to celebrate.

I found a real sense of freedom and authenticity in coming out, and felt like I was able to be completely myself. Others find it brings them closer to the friends or family members that they tell. Of course (and for some this is a priority) it also makes it easier to pursue romantic or sexual relationships with other girls! Being out can also give you the chance to be a role model to younger LGBTQ+ people around you, or simply show them that they aren't alone. It can help you shed feelings of shame around your identity, and avoid the stress of concealing the truth or having to directly lie.

SO, WHY DOESN'T EVERYONE COME OUT?

If coming out can be so great, then why doesn't every LGBTQ+ person do it?

Well, there are a number of possible reasons here too. It might be physically or emotionally safer to be in the closet because of your family, your environment or laws where you are. It could even be because you aren't sure how people will react, or because you want to think about what it means to you on your own for a while first. Some people don't come out at all, and see their sexuality or gender identity as no one else's business.

It is totally okay to not be ready for any reason; even if you know everyone around you will be accepting and supportive, it can still be daunting to take such a big step in letting people know a part of who you are.

On the other hand, it's important to know that coming out doesn't have to feel like locking in your final answer to a question on a TV quiz show. You are allowed to change your mind about the words you use to describe yourself at any point in your life. You don't have to be completely certain of your identity to come out to other people. The first time I told someone I thought I might be gay, I wasn't certain myself. But just saying the words out loud to a friend really helped me feel supported as I continued to figure it out.

HOW SHOULD YOU COME OUT?

Okay, you've decided to come out…
how do you do it exactly?

You can come out at any time, in any place that you feel comfortable, and it doesn't matter if you're sixteen or sixty. There isn't an age limit on coming out. And, similarly, you can do it any way you like. You can do it face-to-face with someone in person. But if you can't (or just prefer not to) do that, you can write them a letter, send them a text, do it by carrier pigeon, write it on a cake – anything goes! And it's also okay not to tell everybody. You can tell just one person, or one small group of people. Coming out doesn't have to mean that suddenly you're out to the whole world at the same time (although throwing a massive coming out party for absolutely everyone you've ever met does sound iconic).

HOW TO PREPARE

It is totally valid to blurt out that you might be gay at a crowded house party with no plan like I did, but some people are a bit less chaotic than 15-year-old me. Here are some ways you can prepare for coming out to other people, especially if you are worried about the reaction you might get:

Try testing the water first. You could bring up an LGBTQ+ celebrity and see what they say.

Think about the time and place that is most comfortable for you, e.g. a public vs private setting, during school hours or afterwards, etc.

Put together a support network. Online LGBTQ+ forums or local LGBTQ+ groups might be useful – they will know what you're going through and might be able to give you advice and support.

Think about (or even practise) what you are going to say if you are worried about doubting yourself or freezing up in the moment. But even if you say something like, 'Umm, well, I think I might be… I mean I definitely am… errr… a… lesbian. I guess? Maybe?'– that's still great. Coming out doesn't have to be like an award-winning movie!

If you're telling your parents or guardians and you're worried their reaction might be negative, make sure to have somewhere you can stay like a friend's house where you can be safe.

Think about how you will answer questions they might have about you and your identity.

COMING OUT... AGAIN?

Coming out is about coming to terms with how you feel about your identity and how you want other people to view your identity.

Because of that, you may have to come out, even to yourself, more than once. It's totally okay to come out as one thing at first, and then later on realise that you've had a shift in your identity and you see your sexuality or your gender differently.

There isn't a limit to the amount of times you can come out.

WHAT IF SOMEONE ISN'T SUPPORTIVE?

Unfortunately, you may have to deal with people who aren't supportive when you come out to them. Here are some suggestions of things to do when dealing with a less-than-enthusiastic reception:

SURROUND YOURSELF WITH AFFIRMING PEOPLE

Before coming out to someone whose reaction you aren't sure about, plan to speak with a friend who is supportive right after. They can help you remember that you are still loved and appreciated.

REMEMBER THAT THERE'S NOTHING WRONG WITH WHO YOU ARE

Intolerance, bigotry and prejudice are wrong, not your identity. Even if this means the end of your relationship with that person, there are still so many people out there who will support you just the way you are.

HELP THEM UNDERSTAND

It may be that the person you come out to doesn't know anything about your identity, and is just confused about what it means. There are lots of videos and articles online, made for exactly this reason, that you could show them to help them understand.

IF YOU WANT, YOU CAN GIVE THEM TIME TO IMPROVE THEIR REACTION

Sometimes in the moment, people can react negatively in a way they don't really mean to. Their concern or worry might manifest as a lack of support, or their own biases and assumptions might come out before they have time to process. If you feel like it, you could talk it through with them once they have had some time to process what you've told them.

'OUTING'

Sometimes it isn't as simple as being able to wait and come out on your own terms.

If other people find out before you are ready – whether because someone you'd confided in told them, or they saw something you'd written in a journal entry or DM – that is called 'outing'. It can be a terrifying experience to lose control of something so personal. If that happens, it's more important than ever to seek out supportive friends and resources to help you through.

We've talked a lot in this section about the first time you come out to someone else, but here's the thing: you won't just come out one time. Even if you put posters up in your neighbourhood saying, 'Hey everyone, I'm bisexual!', you'll eventually meet new people at university, or work, or – I don't know – a weekly crochet club. And you might want to come out to these people, too. The more you do it, the less nerve-wracking it becomes until it just feels as easy as telling people your star sign or your favourite food.

HAFSA

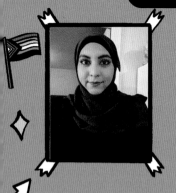

FINDING COMMUNITY

Being visible is so important to me, because I think that as a young, LGBTQ+ Muslim, I had no idea that the community was so vast. You're told that you don't exist, and you end up believing it. When I look at media, I do sometimes see LGBTQ+ people of colour represented, and I might sometimes see an LGBTQ+ Muslim. But there's always a caveat of, 'she's no longer religious and that's the only way she can be truly free – now she has moved away from her faith, she can be queer'. I have very rarely seen someone be of faith and also LGBTQ+ and for it not to be a conflict. You think, 'Well, I'm just the one freak. There can't be any others like me. I'm just going to keep this a secret till I die. I'm not going to ruin this for my family or the people around me. Maybe I was just born wrong.' And then you go into the wider world and you realise, 'No, there's loads of us.' It's just that it's not as safe for many of us to be this visible.

Social media has been amazing at helping me find community. There are so many queer Muslims out there, and there are organisations such as Imaan, Hidayah and London Queer Muslims that connect all of us across the world. It's amazing the way that they create virtual spaces for us to talk to each other. Many Muslims like myself want to be in a faith-based space where we can talk about our religion without feeling that at some point, someone's going to say, 'Oh, yeah and also LGBTQ+ people are going to hell.'

No one is owed your time. No one is owed your space. I think especially when you're young, you feel like you want to get on with everyone. As you get older, you realise that not everyone is good for you, not everyone is worth your energy. And it's totally fine to walk away from those people if it will ultimately be better for you.

I have people in my life who accept me for exactly who I am, and have never queried my existence. They've never asked me for my queer credentials. They've never asked me. 'Well, how many people have you slept with? Are you truly liberated?' They've never told me I should take my hijab off because then I'll be truly free. I've reached out and built my own family of awesome queer people, of queer people of faith, of queer people of colour. And I feel welcomed by everyone.

FAITH & IDENTITY

My parents passed away some time ago, so it's just been me, my brother and my sister. Faith held me together as a human being. It helped me.

It was like the glue that kept me together. Otherwise, I would have totally fallen apart. I guess you could say everyone needs something to believe in. Whether that's faith, whether that's community – for me, it was religion. It gave me higher purpose because it was like, 'I might be falling apart, but I believe in God and I believe I'm here for a reason.'

It can be really difficult to find community when you're an LGBTQ+ Muslim, because in the faith-based community, you're told that being LGBTQ+ is just not allowed. But more than that, you're told that you don't exist. Time and time again, I'll hear, 'Well, that's just not possible,' as if you're some mathematical quandary, or some weird puzzle that doesn't make any sense.

And then when you go into the LGBTQ+ spaces, a lot of people had a lot of negative experiences with religion and with faith. Whilst I completely understand that people can have religion and faith-based trauma from being rejected, from being treated awfully from things like conversion therapy – which is just torture – they sometimes project those experiences onto other people. Instead of me being treated as a person, I'm treated as the representative for my entire religion. I feel that I almost have to announce my queerness in the space, because every single space I've been into that's LGBTQ+, I've been asked if I'm straight or an ally. This happened at Birmingham Pride, London Pride and UK Black Pride.

SELF-CARE & ACTIVISM
When I was first getting into activism, I remember meeting Ruth Hunt, the former head of Stonewall, and I said to her, 'Do you have any advice?'

She replied, 'Yeah. Take a break – because if you keep working and working and working, you will burn yourself out.'

We need activists who can continue to be activists, and not people who have an amazing year and then can't do any more because it's just too much.

We need to help more people become activists, because so many young people think it has to be this massive thing. You need to have a degree. You need to be well spoken. You need to be able to talk about the intricacies of intersectionality perfectly. But really, you just need to be able to step forward and say, 'This is what my life has been. I don't want people to treat me like this. Let's be nicer to each other.' The reason I talk about myself a lot is not narcissism, but because when people see a human example, it can help change their mind.

CHAPTER FOUR
Dealing with Difficult Bits

Being queer is honestly a wonderful gift. But there are also some difficult things that we queer girls go through. Don't worry – we're going to talk through them here, and then we'll look at how to deal with them.

LGBTQ+ PREJUDICE

Prejudice and discrimination against LGBTQ+ people can manifest on an individual level (when two people interact with each other) or a wider social level (including laws, taboos or cultural assumptions).

HOMOPHOBIA
A feeling of hostility, disdain or prejudice against gay people.

Example: Being called a homophobic slur

BIPHOBIA

A feeling of hostility, disdain or prejudice against bisexual people.

Example: The assumption that bisexual people just 'can't make up their mind' or are 'greedy' for being attracted to more than one gender.

TRANSPHOBIA

A feeling of hostility, disdain or prejudice against trans people.

Example: Someone insisting a trans girl isn't 'really' a girl and deliberately calling her by the wrong name and pronouns.

SEXISM

Sexism is a form of prejudice and oppression rooted in the (ridiculous but dangerous) belief that men are superior to women. Let's be honest – this won't be news to you. 'Everyday sexism' is sadly common-place and you may well have experienced at least one of these examples in your life already. You might have tried to stand up for yourself and been called bossy, 'difficult' or a diva for doing it. It's been said that there is nothing teen girls could like that wouldn't then be mocked – whether it's being called a 'fake geek girl' for liking comic books, or people looking down on 'crazy fan girls' who love boybands. As soon as you become aware of this attitude, you see it all over. Here are some examples of sexism.

GATEKEEPING
The idea that girls shouldn't or can't do certain things just... for being girls, apparently?

DOUBLE STANDARDS
The classic (and depressing) idea that if a man sleeps with a lot of women he's a 'stud' or a 'player', but if a woman does the same she's a 'slut'.

TRADITIONAL WOMANHOOD
The idea that all girls should aspire primarily to marriage and motherhood.

SCHOOL DRESS CODES
Rules that specifically police the bodies of girls so they don't 'distract' male pupils, or even teachers, e.g. banning girls from wearing tops that 'expose' their shoulders or collar bones.

SEXUALISATION
Being cat-called (having sexual things yelled at you in the street), groped and seen primarily as a sexual object, or pressured into having sex.

LACK OF RESPECT
When a woman's worth is based on their proximity to men (e.g. using 'that's someone's sister/daughter' as the only reason to respect a woman, or men only backing off if you say you have a partner, even if you've already said you aren't interested).

Misogyny can tie into your other experiences
and identities, for example:

Misogynoir: the unique form of anti-Black racist and sexist
oppression experienced by Black women.

Transmisogyny: the combination of transphobia and misogyny
towards trans women and transfeminine people that creates a form of
oppression not fully shared by either cisgender women or trans men.

Transmisogynoir: the unique form of racism and transmisogyny
that Black trans women face from cis people, as well as other queer
and trans people.

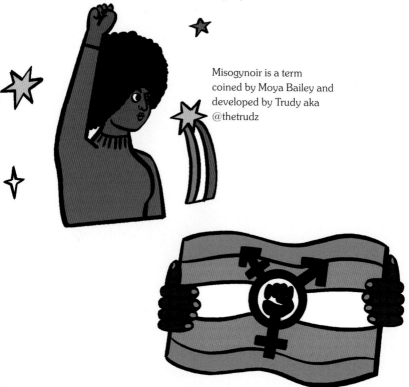

Misogynoir is a term
coined by Moya Bailey and
developed by Trudy aka
@thetrudz

Transmisogyny is a term coined by Julia Serano.

These intersections of prejudice or discrimination can result in their own particular struggles, injustices or dangers.

For queer girls, our experience with sexism can be tied together with our sexuality. Young lesbians might see themselves treated as merely a fetish by men used to watching 'girl-on-girl' porn. I can't remember the amount of times men have claimed they could 'turn me' when I tell them I'm gay, as if I don't know my own identity, or that they are entitled to see me as a sexual object before seeing me as a person. Butch, masculine or otherwise gender non-conforming girls deal with the idea that they aren't behaving how women 'should', and are often shamed for it.

You might also experience 'internalised' versions of misogyny, homophobia, biphobia or transphobia; having absorbed these harmful societal ideas, you might then come to dislike and judge yourself, or other people with your identities, because of it.

Sometimes it can be difficult to separate your real feelings from the things you've been told.

As we look to stand up against prejudice and discrimination, it's vital to help people around us with the issues that affect them specifically, as well as our own limited experiences. Gathering a group of friends who understand and can empathise – and who you can offload to when something bad like the earlier examples happens – is a great way to feel supported. You might also want to tackle these issues together directly. We'll talk about activism in a later section, but we can see through history how the lives of girls have improved through those who stood up to make change happen – and there's no reason you couldn't be a part of that too.

There's not just one way to be a girl, and every girl deserves respect and control over her life, body and choices.

CHAPTER FIVE
Dealing with Bullies

I was bullied for being a lesbian before I even knew I was gay. I'm not going to lie – that was a wild ride.

It started when a guest workshop leader came to a class at my school and asked us to play a 'quick game'. We pushed our desks to the side of the room, and then she read out a series of statements. If we agreed with a statement, we went to one side of the classroom. If we disagreed, we went to the other. I'm sure that she thought it would be a fun and thought-provoking exercise to show that people have all different kinds of opinions, but, as I'm sure you've figured out... that's not what happened. I only remember one of the statements: 'If my friend came out as gay, I would stop hanging out with them'. I was the only one who disagreed. To a class full of 12-year-olds who mostly either didn't know what being gay was, or had been told it was something bad, my response did not go over well. At the end of the lesson, the teacher pulled me aside. Quietly, as if it was a secret, she told me she was proud of me – but other than that, the adults in the room didn't acknowledge what had happened, in the moment or afterwards.

Some of the students, on the other hand, didn't let it go. They spat homophobic insults at me in the hallways and stopped talking when I walked into the room. They spoke openly in classroom discussions about how they thought gay people being able to have children was disgusting – and the teachers did nothing to stop it.

Luckily, I came to the conclusion long before then that there was nothing wrong with gay people, and that everyone should be treated equally.

At the time I didn't realise I was gay myself, so it was more a hypothetical about how to treat other people. I remember being so annoyed at my bullies for thinking being gay was an insult, and I was worried for the next person they decided to target who might be more unsure or confused. But if I'm honest, even when you know there's nothing wrong with being gay, you also know that these bullies mean it as an insult – they see you as something wrong. And that can really mess you up.

Bullying can take a number of forms, including being verbally harassed, being made to feel deliberately left out and excluded, physical violence and more. Homophobic or biphobic bullying is someone doing these things because of your sexuality, such as using slurs or threatening to out you. Similarly, transphobic bullying is acting this way towards trans people because of their gender identity. Bullying might come from someone else at your school, a family member, a co-worker or even someone you considered to be a friend. Bullying can massively affect the people on the receiving end – it might make them feel anxious, depressed or isolated. It can make people scared to go to school, or push them to avoid social situations where the bully might be.

People are bullies for different reasons, and the impact and actions of bullies is a huge spectrum. Some might say offensive things out of ignorance about LGBTQ+ people. Others were taught hatred by their family or upbringing, and don't realise that what they were taught is wrong. Some might be lashing out because it makes them feel good to feel powerful. But just because someone might have a reason to be a bully, that doesn't excuse their actions or the impact they have on others.

One of the most difficult things to deal with when it comes to bullying is that a lot of the advice you're given can feel completely useless. It often focuses on how the bullied person can try to make the bully stop. 'Just ignore them' and 'don't let them see you're upset' is more than likely not going to stop anyone, and has the added bonus of downplaying the very valid and understandable emotional reaction you might have to being bullied. So, instead of repeating these trite phrases, I'm going to suggest something different.

You shouldn't have to change who you are for the sake of bullies – and something I cannot stress enough is that IT IS NOT YOUR FAULT.

You have done nothing to deserve being bullied. You can't force someone to act like a good person – that has to come from them. It's also not your responsibility to stop someone from abusing you.

If you have a school, college or workplace that has useful anti-bullying policies, that's great. In that scenario, you might want to keep evidence or a log of the bullying. If there is someone who can help your situation like a teacher, relative or manager, you can tell them what's been happening. But sometimes that's not possible, especially if your environment or family isn't supportive of LGBTQ+ people.

The effects of bullying include a feeling of powerlessness and the deterioration of your self-worth and confidence. It might help to figure out how to alleviate these effects. Here are some ways to cope if you're being bullied.

If your self-worth is slipping, can you gain confidence by pursuing your passions and creative outlets?

If you are worried about your safety, can you tell someone with the power to help?

If the bully is trying to make you feel ashamed of who you are, can you gain perspective by interacting with other queer people who will celebrate your identity?

Feeling more confident and happier with my identity and community made homophobic bullying, that was supposed to make me feel ashamed of being gay, much easier to deal with. On top of that, having someone in your corner – such as a friend (whether online or in person) – to confide in can help you feel less alone and more in control of your story. And, you can be that person for any friends you have that are being bullied themselves.

Sometimes people think of bullying as a stereotypical image of a child in a school playground, pushing another kid to the ground. While some bullying can look like that, nowadays many people can experience bullying online. Online bullying can feel relentless, because it is 24/7 access – however, there are ways to cut yourself off from abuse that are instantaneous. Have a look at the features of the social media you use, such as block and mute buttons, the ability to go private, disabling anonymous messaging and reporting accounts.

CHAPTER SIX
Looking After Your Mental Health

Looking after your mental health on a day-to-day basis is so important. Too many of us wait until it gets bad before we think to do anything about it. It's like a cup slowly filling up with water — as long as the water isn't spilling over then it's fine, right? We turn around to try and ignore the cup for a minute, but by the time we turn back, the water has already reached the top. But then the tap is stiff and won't turn off and the water is spilling onto the floor and, oh my God, is that an electric socket???

Some stress or worry is part of everyday life – things might go wrong, or we might have to deal with big changes that make us feel unbalanced. And, there is such thing as healthy stress, known as eustress, which can motivate us to focus on goals or tasks that are important to us. Worrying can also show that we care about the person or thing we are worried about. But when these feelings start to get in the way of our everyday lives – and our ability to enjoy them – that can become a real problem.

I've struggled with my mental health all my life, from OCD to anxiety and depression, but my brain's got me through it all! I muddled along during my school years, not really sure what to do about what I was feeling inside, the overwhelming panic I would sometimes get or the intrusive thoughts that wouldn't go away. We weren't taught anything about mental health in our lessons, and I had to figure out ways to get through on my own.

I thought I was doing better during my first year of uni. I was out and proud, making great friends and having new experiences – these were meant to be the best years of my life, right? But then someone I'd met through my queer activism died suddenly, and I sank into a pit of depression. I couldn't get out of bed to shower, let alone make it to my classes. A lot of people see depression as sadness, but for me it was emptiness – a vacuum sucking in all sensation, except the feeling of being slowly overwhelmed. I took some time off and postponed my exams while I got treatment, and it was the best decision I made.

Mental health care is vital for everyone, but studies show young LGBTQ+ people can be even more affected by mental health issues than their straight and cis peers. This isn't because being queer automatically makes you depressed or anxious, but more to do with difficult experiences many queer people face growing up. Being surrounded by people who don't support your identity, being forced into the closet or being bullied for who you are can take a mental toll, and that's on top of worries everyone else is dealing with. If you have issues with internalised homophobia, biphobia or transphobia, you might struggle to be kind to yourself – but remember that you deserve happiness.

Although many warning signs for mental health issues are what you might expect (feelings of helplessness, panic or a lack of enjoyment for things you normally love doing), you might also have other symptoms (like forgetfulness or confusion), or even physical signs (like head and stomach aches or fatigue). Looking after your mental health may look different to different people. Some find meditation or mindfulness exercises helpful, others use journalling and some people need the help of medication from their doctor. Just like your physical health, needing help doesn't make you broken or weak. In fact, there's a huge amount of strength in knowing you're worthy of happiness, especially if you're in an environment that makes you feel lesser.

If you have issues with internalised homophobia, biphobia or transphobia, you might struggle to be kind to yourself – but remember that

You deserve

HAPPINESS.

MAZ

Dear reader, I would like you to imagine me at 14, sporting too much eyeliner and listening to Linkin Park. Imagine me as I spend every waking moment trying to be good – that means academically excellent and well-behaved. More than that, I feel that in my heart, which is bursting with desires I couldn't bear to name – good also means straight.

My secondary school was very white; I was one of three people of colour in a year-group of about 200. In this environment, where you could spot my dark skin and relaxer-fried hair across a crowded dining room, I was very aware of being both observed and ignored. If my academic performance was less than perfect, there was a lot of concern, but my distress went largely unremarked upon. I was everyone's star student, but I wasn't really anyone. I didn't know how to make a space for myself, or that there was even a self to make space for.

Poetry became that space. I could not tell you the first poem I knew; my parents filled our house with poetry, buying collections and anthologies from charity shops and encouraging me and my siblings to read to one another. I became familiar with Robert Louis Stevenson and Spike Milligan before Enid Blyton, read Percy Shelley before Jacqueline Wilson. By my teens, this grew into an obsession with song lyrics, and I turned songs over and over in my head until I knew every syllable like the back of my hand.

When my feelings became too much, I would recite fragments of *The Lady of Shallott* by Alfred, Lord Tennyson or *Daffodils* by William Wordsworth. I wrote them down in notebooks, alongside lyrics from songs by Nightwish or the Red Hot Chilli Peppers. Before I knew it, I was adding fragments of my own. I had always written poetry, stories in verse based on nursery rhymes or bible stories. But this was different – darker and messier. This had neither narrative, point, nor attempt at coherence. On the blank space of a page, in the blank moments between homework and bed, I could write out my anger and my pain and confusion. In the quiet solitude, I was neither watched nor judged; my only limit was what I dared. On those pages, I turned whoever I couldn't stop thinking about into an angel or the sun, or the dawn or a demon. I imagined myself as a ravening monster, or a condemned sinner, anything to make sense of a mind I couldn't control anymore.

Over the years, I learned to be kinder. On those pages I learned to desire without shame and imagine the people I loved as people, rather than symbols of my salvation or damnation. Poetry taught me who I

am and how to live with them. The lesson is
incomplete, but it is everything.

Let's flash back again a moment and imagine me
again at 14. Once again listening to Evanescence
and Panic! at the Disco, once again with bad eyeliner and worse hair.
Imagine the mornings spent in the school library, listening to my
friends talk about youth theatre. They talked about being out of the
watchful gaze of parents and teachers, amongst directors and group
leaders who guided them without restricting them, who let them imagine
lives and scenarios that seemed positively scandalous at the time. I
joined them, as soon as I got my parents on board.

Dear reader, it was everything I dreamed.

Theatre gave me space to have emotions and act on them. Any time I
got into character I could do the unkind thing, the cruel thing, the
ungenerous thing and be rewarded for it. In youth theatre, I could escape
being a girl – with its expectations of heterosexual good behaviour
– to be Van Helsing, or Aladdin in a panto, or an entirely genderless
narrator. On stage, it didn't matter that I failed at performing white
femininity, because my deep voice and expansive stage presence and
masculine mannerisms were assets. On stage, I could fall in love with
Jasmine and be applauded for it. On stage, I could be applauded. I could
be seen by an audience that adored rather than judged. Youth theatre,
with its amateurish enthusiasm and creative freedom, was a way for me
to be seen outside the panopticon of living whilst Black and queer.

In the years after I left youth theatre, poetry continued to sustain
me, to give me a reason to face tomorrow. It gave me spoken word, where
I rediscovered a love of performance and found home behind a mic. It is
only recently that I have found my way back to theatre. Ten years on,
it is still everything I dreamed, still a way for me to be seen without
being controlled, still an escape from the constricting expectations
of racist patriarchy. The difference is, today I step on stage as a poet
with an intimate knowledge of themself. Today, I stand behind a mic as a
bisexual in all their power, as a queer without apology or obfuscation.

Dear reader, today I don't need to hide.

CHAPTER SEVEN
Dating & Romance

Even if you've never gone on a date or kissed anyone before, you can still identify with whatever sexuality you feel is right. You don't need any particular experiences to know who you are attracted or not attracted to, and it doesn't make you any less gay, bi or queer. After all, straight girls don't have to get a boyfriend before they can really call themselves straight, right?

Now here's the part where we talk about a bit of frustrating news that I'm pretty sure you've already figured out: you have to find someone who is not only interested in dating girls, but is interested in dating you, and you need to like them back. Plus, you may have to negotiate how 'out' you both are to friends, family or colleagues – who do you want to tell, and does that match up to your partner's comfort levels and expectations?

If you do like all genders, you need to find someone who will respect that part of your identity.

Rom-coms and romance novels tell us that straight people can find each other just about anywhere, from a coffee shop to the library, or even in the midst of a zombie apocalypse. A straight girl sees a boy and the rules of heteronormativity mean it's 'safe to assume' he's going to be straight. All that's standing in their way is whether he feels that spark of attraction to her too. When you're gay, it doesn't feel that simple. When I was younger, I spent a lot of time scared that I would never find anyone because the odds of finding another queer girl randomly at a coffee shop, let alone a girl I felt something for, seemed so impossible. But there are ways of meeting potential girlfriends that don't rely on the Hollywood narrative idea of romance, but which can be just as magical.

I'm going to talk more about where to meet other queer people in How to Find Queer Spaces from page 90, and every place in that list is somewhere you may well find someone you'd like a relationship with too. There are dating apps specifically for queer girls, online queer communities, LGBTQ+ groups and societies and friends of friends. Even without all that, you might still meet a girl you like somewhere unrelated to LGBTQ+ spaces, and if you don't know if she might be into you too, all you have to do is ask! (Easier said than done, I know, but until we start to be able to read minds, open communication is our only option – and think about how great it could turn out if she says yes!).

You don't have to be publicly out to start dating – that's a conversation to have with your partner to make sure you're both safe and comfortable. So I thought I'd give some cute date examples for any scenario.

PUBLIC

Visit a gay bookshop together and pick out a book for each other

Visit a gay bar or club for an evening date if you're old enough

Pack up a picnic and have a relaxing afternoon in the sun

Find some nature to explore – whether it's a full-on hike or just a stroll in the park together

Try something new together, like a class or activity

Try a classic: dinner and a movie

PRIVATE

Cook a recipe you've never
tried before together

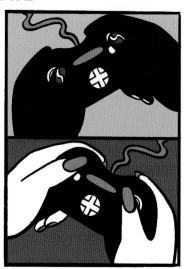

Play a game together
(whether a video game, board
game or even a puzzle)

Get creative with some
arts and crafts

Build a blanket fort and watch a
movie together inside

LONG DISTANCE

Send each other a date night/care package box and unbox them together

Plan a remote movie night with webcams on and cinema snacks

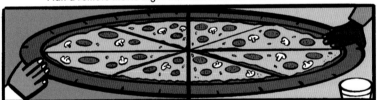

Order food for each other and have a surprise dinner date

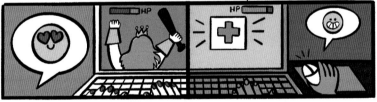

Play an online two-player game while you chat

Create a mixtape playlist for each other and listen together

One of the best things about being queer is that you don't have to be tied to any expectations. The 'rules' of dating in our society generally assume a couple will be a cis woman and a cis man, and 'a man always asks out the woman' or 'a man always pays the bill' kind of fall apart when you're both women. Like, are neither of you meant to pay? Do you just get out of paying the bill at a fancy restaurant by default? Sadly, no. But it does expose how ridiculous so many of these expectations are! (Head to Chapter 10 on page 82 to read about consent and communication.)

Once you've found a partner, here are some things to think about when building a healthy relationship:

TRUST

COMPROMISE

INDEPENDENCE

RESPECT

SUPPORT

FUN

RESPECT

You respect each other's boundaries and expectations, e.g., your time, bodies and emotions.

You know you both have a right to privacy.

Your partner respects your identity, e.g., always using your correct pronouns.

You respect each other's cultural and religious beliefs.

INDEPENDENCE

You have your own friendships, hobbies and identity outside of the relationship.

You feel free to develop and grow as a person separately from the relationship.

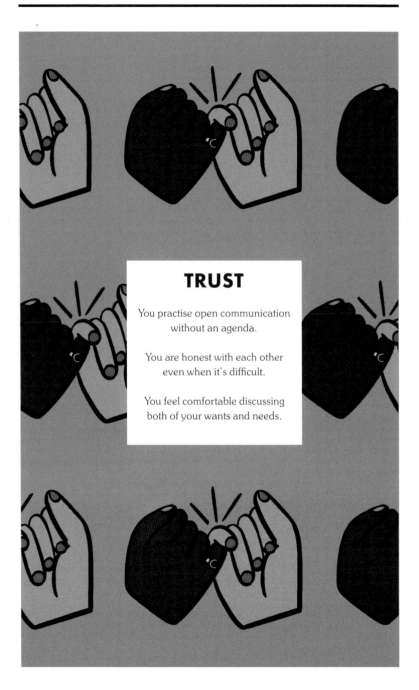

TRUST

You practise open communication without an agenda.

You are honest with each other even when it's difficult.

You feel comfortable discussing both of your wants and needs.

COMPROMISE

You discuss issues and
disagreements calmly
and with respect.

You allow for differences of
thought and opinion.

You both have equal power and
say in the relationship.

SUPPORT

You encourage each others' dreams and goals.

You both support each other in developing as people.

You feel validated and encouraged by your partner.

FUN

You feel happy and valued.

You spend quality time together that you both enjoy.

There is humour and kindness in the relationship.

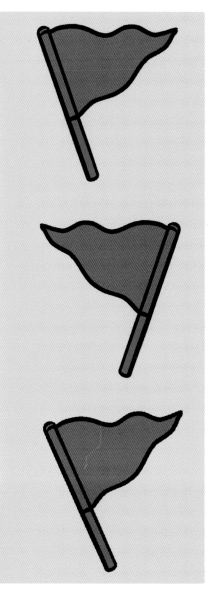

SOME SIGNS OF AN UNHEALTHY RELATIONSHIP

Control,
like dictating how
you dress or act.

Isolation,
like turning you
against your friends.

Physical violence,
like kicking or punching.

Verbal abuse,
like name-calling or
using slurs and insults.

Intimidation,
like shouting at you rather than
communicating calmly.

Dishonesty,
like cheating on you.

Lack of respect,
like ignoring
boundaries you've set.

Ridicule,
like making fun of your interests.

In the next couple of chapters we're going to be talking about sex, relationships and consent. If you're not ready to read about that, or just don't want to, then feel free to skip to page 88 where we'll be talking about finding community.

CHAPTER EIGHT
What 'Counts' as Sex?

You know we talked earlier about the silly expectations around dating? Well, the same goes for sex, too. For some people, there is an expectation that sex is when a man puts his penis in a woman's vagina. Any other stuff going on is just foreplay leading up to the 'main event', and then it's over when the man comes. This is all complete and total nonsense. The idea that penis-in-vagina sex (sometimes referred to as PiV) is the only 'real' sex is just not true, and it gives us a pretty messed up idea about whose pleasure is important in a relationship.

In the UK, underage sex is against the law. The law says that you must be over 16 to have any kind of sexual activity with another person. Any relationship should be consensual and not abusive. The law exists to protect young people from abuse.

Ultimately, what 'counts' as sex is personal and changes from person to person. That lack of universal certainty might seem intimidating – yet another thing you have to work out for yourself – but it can be extremely freeing too. It means there may be types of sex you are 'expected' to want or enjoy that you can decide to never do. You might even identify as somewhere on the asexual spectrum and realise you don't really want to have any kind of sex at all. That autonomy over your own body is entirely valid and should be supported by any partner you have.

So, what kind of things might someone consider to be sex as a queer girl? Well, considering that queer girls themselves might be trans, intersex or cis – and can have all kinds of bodies, genitals and partners – pretty much any kind of sex there is! It's worth noting that some girls refer to their genitals and bodies with different names for their comfort – if in doubt, just ask. Consider this list to be a menu of sorts. Like at a restaurant, this menu is just a list of possible choices – you can order a few different courses, try some of your partner's dishes, and you can get something different next time.

ORAL SEX

Stimulating your partner's genitals with your mouth, lips or tongue. Other words you might hear for different versions of this include: going down on someone, eating someone out, cunnilingus, giving a blow job or rimming (amongst others).

DIGITAL PENETRATION

Otherwise known as fingering. Any time someone is penetrating someone else with their fingers. Two people using their hands to stimulate each other's genitals at the same time is known as mutual masturbation.

PENETRATIVE VAGINAL SEX

Any sex that involves putting something into your (or someone else's) vagina, including sex toys or a penis.

PENETRATIVE ANAL SEX

Similar to penetrative vaginal sex, but involving someone's anus.

NON-PENETRATIVE SEX

This might include things like intercrural sex, 'dry humping' or hand jobs – sex where nothing is going inside anyone else.

SCISSORING

Okay, so scissoring is technically a form of non-penetrative sex. I'm giving it its own section because it's the most talked about sex act/position for queer women – but it's not for everyone. The idea with scissoring is that two people with vulvas intertwine their legs (like two pairs of open scissors coming together) until their vulvas are touching. Then a lot of grinding and rubbing ensues. A lot of people talk about it like it's the thing lesbians always do to have sex, but for some the position is uncomfortable or awkward – they might prefer the same general action but against each other's thighs (or other body parts) instead.

CLITORIS-FOCUSED SEX

A lot of people with vaginas find it hard to orgasm without some form of clitoral stimulation and for some couples, this is the basis of their sex lives, with no penetration at all. It might be with a partners' fingers, other parts of their body or a sex toy.

MUFFING

A digital penetration technique that involves stimulation of the inguinal canals.

You might enjoy one or a mix of these things, or maybe even different things with different partners over your life. There are no rules!

Alongside or instead of sex, there might be other types of touch that are important to your intimacy: kissing, cuddling, licking, comfort, affection and more lingering sensual touch.

You might want to use toys on yourself or your partner to add some fun and variety into your sex life (although they definitely aren't a requirement). Toys you might want to explore include:

A dildo: a sex toy designed for penetration.

A strap-on: a dildo that can be attached to a person using a harness to use for vaginal, anal or oral sex.

A butt plug: a sex toy designed specifically for anal penetration.

A vibrator: a sex toy that vibrates, and is used on or in the body, to enhance sexual pleasure and stimulation.

The types of sex we've talked about so far are all very hands-on, but what about if you're long-distance, or want to fool around while you're not in the same place? Talking on the phone, messaging online and sending photos are all options for many queer people, particularly if they don't have a safe place at home to bring their partners. However, if you're under 18, it's important to learn about the laws where you live. In a lot of places, sending an explicit photo to a partner, even one you've taken yourself, may be considered to be child pornography.

So, what happens when you're ready to have sex for the first time?

CHAPTER NINE
First Times & Having Fun

Here's the thing about virginity – it's kind of made up.
A big deal has been made about virginity, particularly
women's virginity, over the years. Historically, it
often decided your value in a potential marriage,
determined the state of your morality and imbued you
with an imagined innocent purity. It's talked about in
transactional terms – being 'taken' or 'given' or 'lost'.
But just think about it for a second – apparently, straight
cis people lose their virginity when a penis goes into a
vagina. So, what happens if a penis isn't involved? Are
those people just permanently virgins until they die?
Seems like a pretty big oversight, to be honest.

However, just because an idea was made up, doesn't mean it doesn't have a real-world effect. Some people don't really think of having sex for the first time as a big deal, and others consider it to be something really important to them. Both of these attitudes (and every one that falls somewhere in between) are totally valid. What's important to remember is that your worth doesn't suddenly diminish once you have sex.

Communication is key when it comes to sex.

Talking about what you like, don't like or want to try is vital. You can't assume what your partner will enjoy, and they won't be able to guess what you want either. In all likelihood, not everyone you have sex with will be your soulmate, but you should be able to trust them with your body and vice versa – even in a casual or one-off relationship. Every time you're with someone new will be a first time: a new opportunity to discover what they like, and what you enjoy together.

You might have some ideas of what you are 'expected' to do or act like during sex from things like porn. But porn is mostly not like actual sex – it's often not made for women by women, and is designed around what will appeal to straight men watching instead. Porn actors are paid performers, with studio lighting and a script to follow – definitely not the same as most people's sex lives. Sex, especially the first time, might be a bit awkward or messy, but it can also be fun and exciting. You and your partner are in it together and you both want to make yourselves and each other feel good, so just let them know what you like and go from there.

Before you have sex with another person, you might want to try masturbating if you haven't already. Masturbation was never acknowledged in school sex-ed classes at my school – it seems they thought that if it was just never mentioned, then girls somehow wouldn't even know it existed. The idea that masturbation is for teenage boys is pretty popular in our society, but that's totally ridiculous. It's absolutely normal for young (and old) people of any gender to masturbate. It can allow you to understand more about your own body, and what you like and dislike in a sexual or sensual context. It's nothing to be ashamed of or embarrassed by. And you'll be able to talk to your partners about exactly what you want to try when you're together.

**COMMUNICATION
IS KEY WHEN IT
COMES TO SEX.**

CHAPTER TEN
Consent & Safe Sex

Sex-ed in schools is most often aimed at cis and straight kids. They'll warn of the dangers of STDs, maybe get you to put a condom on a banana so no-one gets pregnant – that kind of thing. And all this might feel pretty irrelevant if you're wondering what two people with vaginas need to do to keep themselves safe. Look online and you will find plenty of people asking if two cis lesbians can even get STDs!

THE ANSWER TO THAT QUESTION IS YES.

Even if both people have vaginas, they can absolutely still transmit STDs through their vaginas touching, fingering, oral sex or sharing sex toys without cleaning them first.

So let's talk about keeping safe during sex...

Protection you might need to use includes:

• Condoms (internal and/or external) for penetrative sex
• Dental dams for oral sex
• Gloves or finger cots for fingering

These are all 'barrier' methods of contraception that form a physical block between you and your partner's body.

Before using any of these, always check their instructions and ensure you know when to change them to prevent potential transmission between you and your partner. For example, if you're using a dildo, make sure to put a new condom on the toy between partners, and when changing between different body openings on the same person.

Safety during sex is not just about our physical bodies – our emotional health is just as important. At the top of that list when talking about relationships is consent.

Consent is agreement given by both parties. It is vital every time you have sex.

It must be freely and enthusiastically given by someone with full knowledge of what they're agreeing to. Some people have this idea that asking about consent ruins the moment, but if checking in with each other to make sure everyone is happy and excited about what's about to happen 'ruins the moment', then there probably wasn't really a moment to begin with. In fact, telling someone exactly what you want to do with them can be sexy in and of itself!

Ways to communicate consent:

Keep doing that!

Go a bit slower, right there.

ARE YOU OKAY TO TRY THIS NEXT?

JUST LIKE THAT!

IS THIS OKAY?

Do you want me to keep going?

Can I kiss you?

True consent is all about that being in a situation that is:

INFORMED: everyone knows what is being agreed to.

FREELY GIVEN: everyone can just as easily say 'no' as they can 'yes'.

ENTHUSIASTIC: everyone is fully onboard with what is being consented to, rather than just giving in or being worn down.

REVERSIBLE: everyone feels able to change their mind or withdraw consent at any time.

AWARE: everyone is aware of themselves and their surroundings, including being conscious and sober.

Always, always respect when your partner says 'no'. This might be them literally saying to word 'no', but it might also look like:

STOP

Wait...

I'm tired, can we not tonight?

Pushing your hands away

Freezing up

TRYING TO MOVE AWAY

Looking uncomfortable

If in doubt about whether your partner is comfortable, all you need to do is ask. Even better, talk before anything starts to happen and make sure everyone involved knows it's okay to say 'no' at any time, even after something has begun. No-one owes anyone else their body, including if they had previously consented at another time to another type of sex – or even if they'd agreed minutes before. It's totally okay to change your mind, and if someone asks you to stop that should happen immediately.

PART 3

FINDING YOUR COMMUNITY

CHAPTER ELEVEN
Queer Spaces & Friendships

Before you come out, you might be worried about what your friends will think or if this will change anything in your relationship. For a lot of people nothing much changes – your friends might have questions, but they love you and want to support you as you figure out your identity. Unfortunately, some people do experience being ostracised from their friend group simply because of their gender or sexuality.

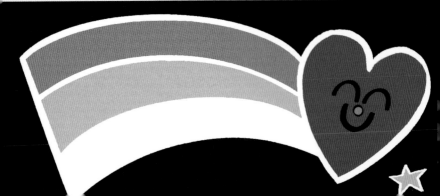

The thing to remember if your relationships do change, is that it isn't your fault, and there are so many people out there who would be lucky to be your friend. Queer friendships and spaces can be amazing because sometimes we have to build our own 'found families' who fill the role of siblings or even parents. Queer people don't necessarily have birth families that share their identity, so we don't grow up learning about our history, culture or community from the start. Instead, we have to learn it where we can, often later in life, from places like this book. Finding our way to queer spaces can help spread and share real stories of queer life, as well as the history of our elders.

There can be an incredible sense of belonging when socialising with other people who understand your identity and experiences – a casual validation that calms the soul. That isn't to say you can't feel accepted by your friends and family who aren't queer, but queer communities can be wonderfully affirming even if you have external support elsewhere. I say 'communities' plural because there isn't just one big community. LGBTQ+ people are just as varied in their interests and personalities as cishet people, after all! On top of that, you might be seeking different queer communities which share other aspects of your identities like religion or race too, to enhance that feeling of understanding and shared experience.

Historically, a woman's place was seen to be in the home at the side of a man, whether it was her father or husband. No, thank you. Spaces for queer women, that served as an escape from both sexism and homophobia, have been vital to our community for decades. That might have been lesbian bars, queer bookshops and cafes, or even activist circles. Before the age of social media and the internet, women found each other in these spaces, utilising pamphlets, posters and papers to communicate. Now, of course, it's a lot easier to find other queer women if you want to – both in online spaces, but also using the internet to find in-person safe spaces for queer people too.

Queer spaces, like community centres, queer businesses or even queer friend's homes, can do more than create a sense of belonging. They also function as potential havens for those with unsupportive home environments. A lot of queer people still worry about being open and out in public (by holding hands with their partner in the street, for example) and that potential anxiety becomes much more manageable in a space where how you feel and express yourself is treated as normal as it should be.

MIKAELA

It starts with a stressed girlfriend. I'm over in Florida from the UK, visiting my partner, Sarah. She's exhausted, and I think we should escape. After some convincing, Sarah agrees, so we pack a little stuff, and drive out to Orlando.

As we listen to queer songs together, peace and tranquility wash over us. I love being with my girlfriend, the most loving, gregarious, loyal person I've known, who sometimes needs a small push to be as generous to herself as she is to those she loves. She lets me push, and we're escaping.

As long as I can remember, I've understood what it means to 'escape'. When I was younger, it was convincing myself (or pretending) I was ill, to avoid school. As I grew up, it could mean visiting a London theatre, or riding roller coasters with fellow theme park enthusiasts.

In the last decade, I left behind some of that ability to just escape when I want to. New circumstances, different relationships, changing expectations and obligations. And coming out as trans; whatever way I want to dress, I can't really escape. Neutral: I'm seen as male, something that I'm not. Femme: still probably not going to be read the way I want to be.

It's so much easier to feel seen for who you want to be with people who know you – or at least know what it's like to be unseen, too. The weekend we escaped to Orlando, I probably felt safer and more seen than I ever have before – a story that'll never stop being a pleasure to tell.

The people who help make this story are Sarah, my friend Paige, and Annie (also in this book!) who I had yet to meet. The day after our drive, we pick a restaurant at a theme park resort. Annie and Paige join us, and we immediately fall into an easy mode of chatting about everything that comes to mind (our first topic is horror movies).

A disfigured trans lesbian and her bisexual girlfriend, a fat bisexual princess and a disabled non-binary Latinx person using a wheelchair. A sight to see, perhaps, an irregular group, and all of us queer, all of us happy.

We grab dinner, but it doesn't feel like nearly enough time, so we pack Annie's wheelchair into the car and drive to another restaurant on the other side of the resort. There's a beach nearby, and hammocks; waiting for a table, we watch over the lake, attempting to fit in a hammock together. Rolling, tumbling, giggling (and posting on Instagram), we try to maintain order, but it's a messy business.

My favourite hammock moment is helping Paige up to her feet. Paige has soft hands. We should touch our friends' hands more often, if we want to, when we can.

Inside the restaurant is excitement and noise. Special drinks are announced with ludicrous fanfare, and we laugh ourselves near-hoarse, and I hold every moment as it hits. Experiences I thought I'd left behind with dropped friends, dead relationships; shedding my old skin. Choosing transition and change didn't ruin me. I've got this, and I've got it better. A fully actualised and equal relationship, and friends who are queer, disabled and marginalised in ways that help us see each other clearer.

No talking at cross purposes, just an innate feeling of rightness. A great time, laughing and enjoying our drinks, griping about ableism and racism and fatphobia and loneliness that affects us, in ways that are safe and loving and good, it helps us feel less lonely.

I love us. And we love every moment, and we're still not done, so we end up at yet another restaurant, back near where we started. We're tired, but it's worth it. We just keep talking, laughing, taking photos, making the most of it all.

When we finally make it back to our cars – whether as a nod to how much our evening has cost us, or just because it takes their fancy – Annie begins to sing Cy Coleman's *Big Spender*. I join in, and Sarah films us. Annie is already becoming one of the best friends a fellow disabled non-binary lesbian could have, even mere hours after I first met her.

My steadfast, luminous girlfriend; my kind, discerning good friend; my powerful, exuberant new friend – a day spent with three wonderful reminders that, for every transition I've made, I could find new, loving people to share my new, loving life with. Becoming the person I am doesn't mean I abandoned hope of escaping the world that wants to squash this improved version of me; I just had to find the people to escape with.

In the car with Sarah driving home, I reflect – with clarity and no hyperbole – on one of the best evenings of my life. I am a lesbian, non-binary trans woman, and I deserve beautiful experiences with beautiful people that I love, and I've had them.

And I will have them again.

CHAPTER TWELVE
How to Find Queer Spaces IRL & Online

I don't think I've ever consciously gone out of my way to make queer friends, yet pretty much everyone I am friends with isn't cishet. I didn't meet any of my friends at specifically gay venues like clubs or bars, or traditional queer events like Pride, either. So how did that happen?

It's not necessarily going to be something you can manufacture by spotting another queer person out in the wild by sight and introducing yourself. After all, you can't assume someone's identity just by looking at them. One possible explanation is a powerful queer magnet hidden somewhere in my body that pulls every gay person within 100 metres towards me, but I'm sure the MRI I had as a teenager would have picked that up. It's much more likely that me being the very out and proud person I am allowed other queer people to feel comfortable around me (and probably put a lot of potential homophobes off too)!

You don't necessarily have to go to queer-specific spaces to find queer friends – we are pretty much everywhere.

But, maybe you do want to find a larger queer community, for all the reasons in the previous section and some of your own.

You might want to try queer environments where you feel comfortable:

Are you into partying and dancing? Try a queer bar or club night if you're old enough.

A bit of a jock at heart? Lots of cities have queer sports teams you can join.

Do you want to get involved in activism? Check out your local LGBTQ+ society or campaigning group.

Give a local queer youth group a visit.

After something more chill? Look for local queer book clubs.

One of the best things about queer friendships you seek out based on your interests is that unlike a lot of friendships you build as a kid or teenager, they aren't tied to proximity. You don't have to stay just within your school, for example, but can forge your own path to friendship with people who share common interests and hobbies.

If the examples I gave seem a bit intimidating, or you're nervous about coming into a big group of people you don't know, then something like a queer crafting or hobby-based group might be a good option. There's probably a queer community for any hobby you can think of, because LGBTQ+ people's interests are as varied as everyone else's. It gives you something to talk about off the bat, and you can always concentrate on the task at hand if you don't feel up to chatting right away. Or even look at bigger events that reflect your interests, like a comic con, which might have a smaller queer meet up as part of it, and which will be full of people excited to talk about something you love!

Honestly, a lot of the people at these groups and events probably started out just as nervous as you. They've just had a chance to make friends for a bit longer already.

And if there's nothing in your general area… maybe you could think about starting a meet-up or club of your own!

In your area there might also be things like: LGBTQ+ community centres,

bookshops, cafes, museums and archives, faith-based groups, historic queer neighbourhoods or one-off events.

Of course, there are the online spaces too. The very first queer people I spoke to were on LGBTQ+ youth forums, but you might find a community on discord servers, online meet ups, social media, community-based apps and more. I've made some amazing friends through YouTube – chatting online about our shared interests and hyping up each other's videos.

You always want to make sure to protect yourself online, particularly as a queer person, as your considerations might be different to your cishet peers. Here are some things you can do to keep yourself safe:

• Check privacy setting on social media to ensure you don't out yourself with your posts.
• If you're under-18, look for online spaces that are specifically for queer teenagers.
• Utilise the mute/block/report features on the apps you're using to remove any hateful or upsetting messages.

Online friends can be just as special as the people you see every day at school or work, and you may well have opened up to them just as much about your fears or dreams. If you're a queer person living somewhere away from easy access to in-person queer resources, those online friendships can be a crucial lifeline to genuine acceptance.

CHAPTER THIRTEEN
Style and Self-expression

I know a fair few people who, after coming out, really wanted to 'look gay'. They desperately wanted strangers on the street to know this important thing about them that they had finally been ready to share. How could something so fundamental to who they are be unseen by people around them – even people in that same community? I definitely felt a pull to present myself in a way that clued other people (especially other queer people) into the fact I was a lesbian. But I also didn't want to do anything that felt unauthentic to who I was. I didn't want to trade the comfort I'd found in my sexuality with a new discomfort of projecting an outward self that wasn't me. In the end, I ended up buying a lot of patches and pins that celebrated queerness, which honestly... was very gay of me.

Here's the thing: there is no haircut, clothing choice or style which is inherently, universally 'queer'.

There are elements of dress and outward expression which have social connotations of queerness. You might have heard people talk about some of these ideas before – and on the outside, they might seem confusing and arbitrary, like 'lesbians will make anything into earrings!' There's nothing inherently gay about a piece of jewellery, but our community has long used accessory choices to outwardly flag their sexuality to others – from asexual people wearing black rings, to the more recent trend of lesbians donning oversized earrings.

Although jokes about fashion being a sure-fire way to guess someone's sexuality are often told within the LGBTQ+ community, to talk about ourselves, we should remember that they are ultimately just stereotypes. I mean, I do have a collection of massive ridiculous earrings, but that isn't what makes me a lesbian.

For some queer girls, their gender expression and style are a huge part of their queer identity. Labels like **BUTCH** and **FEMME**, for example, have a long history in our community and express a relationship with masculinity or femininity beyond the traditional heterosexual ideals of gender. But you don't have to pick one or the other.

THERE ARE AS MANY WAYS TO EXPRESS YOURSELF AND YOUR IDENTITY AS THERE ARE PEOPLE ON THE PLANET.

One of the things that I've found most liberating in queer spaces is the relaxed attitude I've found to social expectations of gender. As girls and women, there is often an exacting beauty standard placed upon us by what has historically been deemed as attractive in a heteronormative society. It means the pressure to wear make-up or shave our body hair is hard to separate from our own personal desires to do those things. Do I really want to get rid of my leg hair for me, or is it something I only do when other people can see it? I shaved my legs all through my teenage years. To think that I could go outside and someone might see me with even a speck of hair on my legs... was mortifying! But when I realised that I didn't shave them in the winter, a period when I'd wear jeans all the time and I was the only person who would see my legs, I understood: 'Oh, I'm definitely doing this for other people'. When I stopped shaving, I still felt very self-conscious at first. But that summer I went to an LGBTQ+ conference, and I remember sitting in a hotel room with a group of other attendees, all queer women, who were all being so casual about their body hair. Which, you know, makes sense, because it's natural hair that grows on human bodies – but it took seeing other people in my community being their authentic selves for my own confidence to really click.

I identified at that time as being very feminine, specifically as a femme queer woman. I had ideas about what femininity had to be, and shaving your body hair was one of those things that society said made you feminine – it fit neatly into that aesthetic and that identity. So, going to these spaces with queer and gender non-conforming people openly playing around with what gender and femininity means, who taught me that I could decide for myself, felt so liberating and supportive.

I think it's pretty important to note here that this is all from my specific queer point of view (as a white cis queer woman). Your relationship to your body, hair, style and general self-expression may well be affected by other aspects of your identity. You might have different social pressures, feelings about femininity or perceptions of yourself based on the experiences of the body you're in.

If you are not totally ready to come out, you might find utilising community symbols (like wearing the colours of the flag designed for your identity) can feel personally affirming. For some people it's liberating and exciting to show their identity – for example, to get a haircut that makes them feel more identifiably gender non-conforming. But for others, it's more comfortable staying as they are. If you're queer, you're queer enough, regardless of how you present yourself with your looks and style.

It's not something you have to do to be accepted in queer culture and spaces, so don't pressure yourself into changing because of what you think others might expect from you as an out queer person.

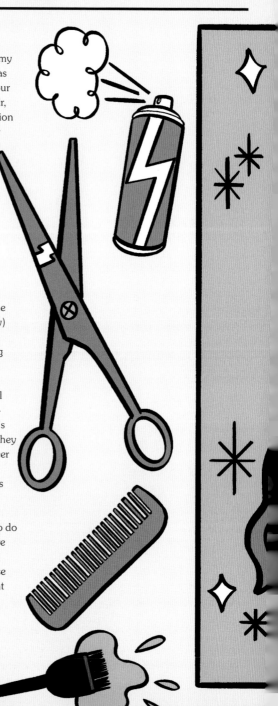

CHAPTER FOURTEEN
See Yourself

I genuinely believe that representation is one of the most powerful tools in both changing public perception of LGBTQ+ people, and also (more importantly) empowering queer people themselves. When done well, films and books that focus on queer lives can open up a window to our experiences. More representation means more windows open, allowing us to peer into the complex and varied lives of others in our community. When real life LGBTQ+ role models rise to prominence in public life, from music to sport, it can help break down mental barrier of things queer people 'can' or 'should' do.

QUEER HISTORY

However, when so much of the mainstream media about queer women wasn't made by queer women, it means that there can be a lot of inauthentic portrayals or harmful tropes. This isn't always the case, but it can feel a bit frustrating when you want to see something that feels real to you, and it ends up just making you want to roll your eyes and switch off the TV. One that always makes me let out a long-suffering sigh is the 'Bury Your Gays' trope, a theme in TV and film that sees queer characters die at a higher rate than straight characters, often to fuel straight characters' motivations or plotlines. There's also the common issue of cis men playing trans women, which enforces the dangerous and false idea that trans women are just men in dresses. Thankfully, there are some great films that focus on queer women out there.

THE TOP TEN ICONIC SAPPHIC FILMS (AS CHOSEN BY ME)

But I'm a Cheerleader
San Junipero (Black Mirror)
Summerland
Saving Face
Princess Cyd
Booksmart

Alice Junior
The Watermelon Woman
Yes or No
Margarita, with a Straw

REMEMBER TO CHECK THE AGE-RANGE OF THESE FILMS BEFORE WATCHING.

But it isn't only mainstream productions or superstar celebrities that give us representation. Queer women have created their own representation in their own communities, both in person and online, for decades. Everything from fan fiction to DIY filmmaking to zines have been used by queer women to explain and explore their sexuality, gender and other identities. These low-budget pieces of creativity don't have to go through the approvals of a big shot producer, who, more often that not, is probably a straight white guy mainly focused on profit.

Instead, they can go straight from you and your friend's brains into action. A short TikTok about your first Pride parade is a piece of representation that you can cast out like glitter, that might find its way to another queer person who needed to see that moment of hope.

So if you find a piece of glitter in the form of a film or webcomic or Instagram account – pass it on.

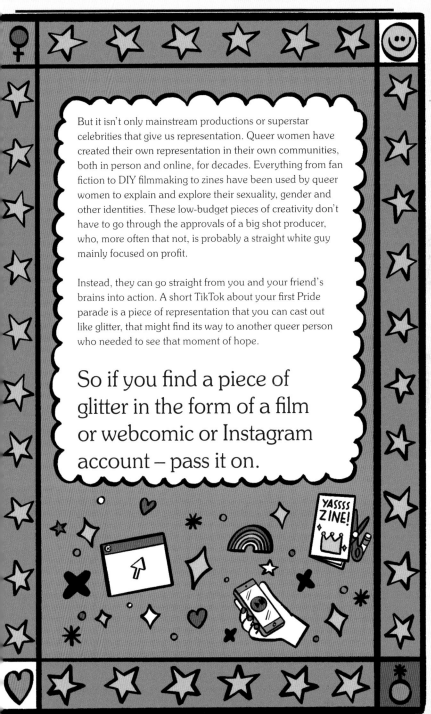

ANNIE

GENDER

When I was going through the process of discovering my gender, I looked back on times when I didn't feel comfortable with presenting myself as feminine, and why that was. Was it because I wasn't cisgender? Or was it internalised misogyny? Eventually I settled into the identity of being non-binary and gender fluid because that's what felt the most authentic and truthful to me. Everyone who has the same kind of gender fluid woman-aligned feeling is going to have different language for it - all I can do is try to convey how it feels inside. Sometimes in my head I think, 'I'm a part-time woman' - I try to play around with the language as much as I can. Like, I'm part of this club, but not exclusively part of this club. I'm a social butterfly at the gender party hanging out in all the spaces.

DISABILITY

My body would hurt all the time and my assumption was this is the human existence - everyone is hurting in this way, and it's me who hasn't built up the stamina to get through it. I brought home my diagnosis of Ehlers-Danlos syndrome (EDS) and it was like another coming out - this is part of me too. I'm permanently, and maybe progressively, disabled. Because of my EDS I have fragile joints and it's hard for me to stand up for long periods of time. For that reason (amongst others) I sometimes use a cane for walking short distances and use a powerchair for anything where I would have to walk or stand for long periods of time. The campaigns I've run have often revolved around representation and education. My advocacy around ambulatory wheelchair users (a wheelchair user with some ability to walk) was often met with online comments like: 'I had no idea' and 'I never thought of that'. When I get that response, it pains me, but I know going forwards they won't be harassing people they see get up from a wheelchair and walk. They might even advocate for that person if they see somebody else reacting the way they used to. It might just be on an individual level, but for me it's a sign of impact and change that representation can initiate in people.

COMMUNITY, INTERNET & DISABILITY

As a young adult living in Miami, after I came out I was able to make friends and be part of a local lesbian community. My social life became active with joyful parties and progressive advocacy meetings. But as my disabilities increased over time, I began to lose my in-person communities because participating in social events became inaccessible to me as a chronically ill wheelchair user. When disability and illness started to create a sense of isolation, it was the disability community on social media that provided that sense of community for me again. Through my advocacy work I got to have discussions with strangers online, but I also gained close friendships where we had so much to bond about and share with each other.

DATING & ROMANCE

One of the tricky things with disability and online dating is the 'coming out' – when exactly do you tell someone you're disabled? Do you put it right on your profile, or do you tell them when you first start messaging, or after your first date? It's going to be different for everybody. I've experimented with my profile, trying to include all the different kinds of truthful photos of myself: standing, using a cane and in my wheelchair. I've experienced ableism from people on dating apps, like, 'you need somebody more responsible than me to take care of you' – like if we go on a date, they will have to babysit me. But I've also had people who are chill about it. There was one person I hadn't told about my disability before we met up. I walked in with the cane, and she didn't say anything about it. Eventually I brought it up and asked, 'Do you want to know about the cane?' I loved her response: 'I mean, yeah, you can tell me if you want, but you don't have to'. It just didn't phase her. It wasn't dismissive, but we just had more interesting things to focus on in that moment together.

REPRESENTATION

As a child, I didn't see queerness as a possibility – I now realise that's a representation issue. I didn't see it as an option around me in my surroundings or in media. It made me feel less likely to fit in and I didn't know how to navigate it. If I had seen more representations of people like me – queer, plus-size, disabled people of colour – I would have felt less antagonistic within myself. **I kept questioning myself.** Is this possible? Is this real? For a long time, I thought you had to present as androgynous to be non-binary – and I don't read as androgynous at all – so I worried people wouldn't accept me because of that. The first time I saw someone who felt like me was in a movie called *Mosquita Y Mari*, and I cried. I saw it when I was already an adult, but I never saw a character like that growing up. <u>Representation makes you feel like your existence is possible.</u>

I hate it, because it's so cliche, but if you are feeling isolated in your experiences, I hope you can take a look at this book and know you do have a community of people who care about you. There will be people who will treat you with kindness and respect, even if they aren't a part of your life right now.

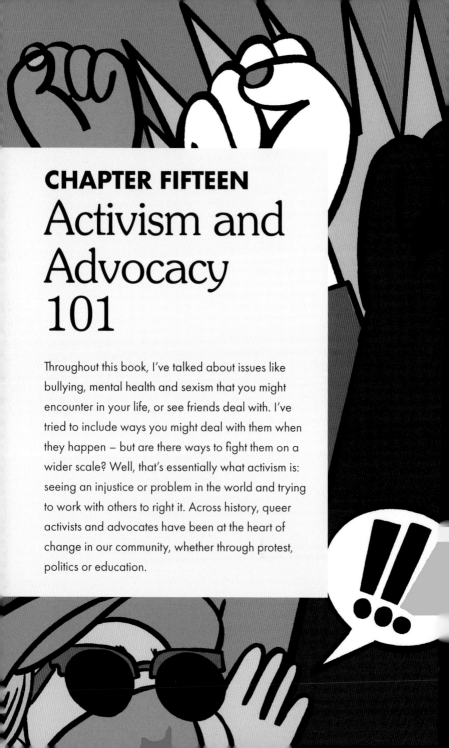

CHAPTER FIFTEEN
Activism and Advocacy 101

Throughout this book, I've talked about issues like bullying, mental health and sexism that you might encounter in your life, or see friends deal with. I've tried to include ways you might deal with them when they happen – but are there ways to fight them on a wider scale? Well, that's essentially what activism is: seeing an injustice or problem in the world and trying to work with others to right it. Across history, queer activists and advocates have been at the heart of change in our community, whether through protest, politics or education.

My first experience of queer activism was at school... and I had absolutely no idea what I was doing. The school computers wouldn't allow students to access certain websites if the system detected something the administration had determined as 'inappropriate'. The reason for the site being blocked was displayed on the screen with an error message: contains nudity, contains drugs, contains defamatory language – that kind of thing. Well, one lunchtime, I tried to access the Stonewall charity website and up pops a message:

Blocked for lesbian and gay content

NOT OK

I knew homophobia was rife amongst people at my school – I'd experienced it – but something about such blatant homophobia on a structural level knocked me sideways. I tried some other websites I knew, like LGBTQ+ charities and support sites for young people. All of them were blocked. A small optimistic part of myself hoped it was a mistake; it was still unacceptable that the blocking software had this option – but maybe the school hadn't thought to check what exactly it was blocking? I knew I had to do something about it. I scheduled an appointment with the head teacher with some friends, thinking maybe it would all be sorted out quickly. Yeah... it wasn't.

We were told it was necessary for 'student safety' – as if the safety of LGBTQ+ students didn't come into it – and it was 'just how it was going to be'. We were incensed. Why couldn't she realise how devastating seeing that error page might be for vulnerable queer kids looking for advice or support? A direct meeting with the person at the top hadn't worked, so we decided to ask the students. We visited classrooms during break times explaining what had happened and asked people to sign a petition we had created. We asked the IT team if it would be possible to remove 'lesbian and gay' content from the blocking filter and they confirmed it was possible. We gathered information about the damage homophobia could do to young people. We made another appointment with the head teacher.

I would love to tell you all this work ended with the teachers admitting they were wrong and changing the policy, but sadly that wasn't the case. Instead we were told only students over the age of 16 (who were granted special permission) would be allowed to access the sites – oh, and also that teachers would not be able to identify themselves as being LGBTQ+ supportive in case it led to 'inappropriate relationships'.

It'd be pretty easy to see this as an utter failure. The policy was still in place when we left for university – it felt like we hadn't made a difference at all. Except we had. Policy is not the only way to change things. By being open and vocal about LGBTQ+ rights, we'd spoken to groups of students who otherwise wouldn't have known anyone who was supportive of their identities. We'd started to open up the school to the possibilities of an inclusive environment. A couple of years ago, I was actually invited back to the school to do an assembly for LGBTQ+ History Month and students told me about how much they'd learnt in classes about different genders and sexualities.

So it is absolutely possible for your activism to make changes. No matter if it's in a big or small way, you've got the power to make a difference in someone's life – and there's not just one way to do it. Maybe the thought of having to talk face-to-face in a meeting with an authority figure like I did makes your palms sweat. The good news is, there are so many more ways to get involved with causes you care about. You could:

VOLUNTEER FOR A CHARITY OR ORGANISATION, e.g. volunteering to run LGBTQ+ education sessions with a school outreach organisation.

RAISE MONEY for a charity or group that helps with an issue you care about.

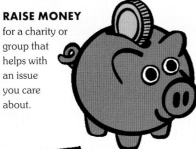

DONATE YOUR SKILLS TO A CAUSE, e.g. volunteering to design some social media graphics for an online campaign.

HELP SPREAD clear and accurate information about an issue to get more people involved.

PROTEST AT MARCHES OR RALLIES, or take part in direct action like sit-ins or walk-outs.

STAND for a position in your university's elections to help represent LGBTQ+ students on a policy level.

Everyone has different skills and levels of comfort. You don t have to be the person with a megaphone speaking to a crowd to change the world.

CHAPTER SIXTEEN
Queer Ladies Through History

The history of queer women is frustratingly difficult to pin down – which made this chapter a real pain to be honest with you all. Queer men often make the history books for the wrong reasons, through court documents and public scandals when gay relationships between men were illegal. However, queer relationships between women have largely not been criminalised, so the issue is more that we often can't point out a sapphic relationship without some sputtering historian claiming they were just Good Friends™.

Queer women have always existed throughout history, all across the world. This timeline is only a tiny fraction of the achievements and events we've been a part of. Hopefully it can serve as inspiration for you to look into the queer history of things you are passionate about – whether it's science, sports, the arts or politics.

Marsha P. Johnson and Sylvia Rivera create the gay, gender non-conforming and transgender advocacy organisation S.T.A.R. (Street Transvestite Action Revolutionaries), which serves homeless and vulnerable members of the community.

Sweden is the first country in the world to allow transgender people to legally change their sex. They also provide free hormone therapy as part of that policy.

1970

1972

The first Pride is held in London, bringing in around 2,000 participants.

One of the first recorded meetings focused around discussions of bisexuality is held by a gathering of Quakers with

Lisa Orlando writes *The Asexual Manifesto*, which is published by the New York Radical Feminists and is distributed within feminist circles.

A small group known as the 'Subarashii onna-tachi' or 'Wonderful Women' become some of the first women to publicly identify as lesbians

in Japan, beginning a trend of queer women publishing small magazines or pamphlets in the following years.

1974   1975

over 130 participants. They issue what becomes known as 'the first public declaration of the bisexual movement' called the 'Ithaca Statement on Bisexuality'.

Angela Morley is the first openly transgender person to be nominated for an Academy Award (for Best Music, Original Song Score/Adaptation for *The Little Prince*).

The first conference for African-American lesbians is hosted under the title 'Becoming Visible' in San Francisco.

Sally Ride is the first LGBTQ+ person to go to space (although we wouldn't know this until 2012, when her obituary revealed her partner of nearly 30 years was a woman called Tam O'Shaughnessy).

1980   1981   1983

Tennis player Billie Jean King becomes the first prominent female athlete to come out as gay.

The Lesbians and Gays Support the Miners group of campaigners is created in support of workers in the miners' strike in the UK.

1984

1988

The world's first bisexual political organisation BiPOL is founded in the USA.

Section 28 is introduced in the UK. It prohibits local authorities and schools from 'promoting [...] the acceptability of homosexuality as a pretended family relationship'.

The World Health Organisation declassifies same-sex attraction as a mental illness.

South Africa becomes the first country to explicitly prohibit discrimination based on sexual orientation in its constitution.

The Sappho group is created to support lesbian, bisexual and trans women in Kolkata – the first of its kind in India.

1992 1996 1999

20,000 women march in the first Dyke March, held in Washington, D.C.

Trans Day of Remembrance is founded in the USA to memorialise those who have died as a result of transphobia. It is now a day of remembrance worldwide.

The Netherlands becomes the first country to legalise same-sex marriage.

The first gay pride parade in the Chinese-speaking world is held in Taiwan, with over 1,000 attendees.

2001   2002   2003

New York passes the Sexual Orientation Non-Discrimination Act, which is the first legislation in the world to officially mention asexuality.

The first ever gay pride parade in a predominately-Muslim country is held in Turkey.

Nepal's constitution becomes the first in Asia to explicitly protect the rights of lesbian, gay, bisexual and transgender people.

Kyrsten Sinema is elected as the first bisexual member of the US Senate.

2015   **2017**   **2018**   **2019**

The first West African LGBT-inclusive religious gathering takes place in Ghana.

Taiwan becomes the first country in Asia to legalise same-sex marriage.

Yasmin Benoit becomes the first openly asexual woman to appear on the cover of a UK magazine, with her cover shoot for Attitude entitled 'The Activists'.

Stephanie Byers, a member of the Chickasaw Nation, is the first Native American trans person elected to office in America.

2019

2020

The Arctic and Antarctic celebrates the first ever Polar Pride Day.

FIVE QUEER WOMEN FROM AROUND THE WORLD YOU SHOULD KNOW ABOUT

KASHA JACQUELINE NABAGESERA

is honestly incredible. She's an activist who has been fighting for LGBTQ+ rights in Uganda since she was a teenager herself. Alongside David Kato, she succuessfully sued the Ugandan magazine *Rolling Stone* for publishing the names of gay people under the title, 'Hang Them'. She opened Uganda's first gay bar, named Sappho Islands in 2010. She's received a number of awards, including the Nuremberg International Human Rights Award, for her work fighting for LGBTQ+ people in her country.

FRIDA KAHLO was a bisexual Mexican artist whose paintings – often self-portraits or with elements of autobiography – were inspired by both indigenous and colonial influences. For most of the general public, Kahlo is known for being the painter with an iconic unibrow – but that is only one snowflake on the tip of her iceberg. I visited one of her homes in Mexico a couple of years ago, where there was an exhibit of her clothing. The leg braces and back corsets put her disability and chronic pain on full display, including how she utilised the garments to aid and conceal her conditions in equal measures.

AKKAI PADMASHALI is a human rights activist from India, working to de-stigmatise and champion equality for trans people. She has a number of 'firsts' under her belt, including being the first trans person in Karnataka to register their marriage, and the first trans person in the whole country to receive a driving licence stating her gender correctly as female. She has spoken across the world about the legal rights of LGBTQ+ people, as well as speaking on the discrimination she's faced herself. She also founded NGO Ondede which trains journalists and law enforcement on gender issues, and well as skills workshops for LGBTQ+ community members.

I first saw **KYLIE KWONG** on Masterchef Australia while at university, and remember being so annoyed I'd never heard of her before! She's a powerhouse of a chef from Sydney, inspired by the Cantonese cuisine taught to her by her mother, as well as a champion of sustainability in the kitchen. I have always admired outspoken queer women whose life's work is centered around fighting for LGBTQ+ rights, or creating art and writing about queerness. But I wanted to include Kylie as an example of someone whose talents are totally separate from her sexuality, because ultimately, every one of us gets to decide what role our queerness plays in our lives.

I might be biased for choosing someone from the UK for my European pick, but how could I not pick **LADY PHYLL** (aka Phyll Opoku-Gyimah)? She is an activist, the co-founder of UK Black Pride, and a ton of other things besides. UK Black Pride promotes unity and co-operation among all Black people of African, Asian, Caribbean, Middle Eastern and Latin American descent, as well as their friends and families, who identify as Lesbian, Gay, Bisexual or Transgender. Since its creation in 2005, it has provided a vital space for the community. It started as a seaside day trip for a small group of members of the online social network Black Lesbians in the UK, and now attracts thousands of participants each year. She's the only person in this list who I've been lucky enough to see speak at an event, and her energy, humour and expertise is infectious.

CHAPTER SEVENTEEN
Queer Symbols Through History

Throughout much of history, queer people had to keep their desires secret, but many still felt a yearning to connect with others like them. So secret slang, symbols and codes were sometimes used to indicate queerness and safety between people in the know. Even now, symbols like the pink triangle – once an emblem used by the Nazis to identify queer men – have been reclaimed as a sign for a queer-friendly space.

One LGBTQ+ symbol I'm 99.9% sure you know about is the six-stripe rainbow flag. The idea of the flag started in the 70s when artist Gilbert Baker created an eight-stripe flag which also included hot pink and turquoise stripes. This was refined to six stripes over the years and it became the symbol we use today. Each colour has its own significance to the LGBTQ+ community:

RED FOR LIFE

ORANGE FOR HEALING

YELLOW FOR SUNLIGHT

GREEN FOR NATURE

BLUE FOR HARMONY OR PEACE

PURPLE FOR SPIRIT

Under the umbrella of 'queer girl', there are a number of identities you might hold – and each may have their own symbols and flags.

PROGRESS PRIDE

Designed by Daniel Quasar, it combines the six-stripe flag, the trans flag, and brown and black stripes to represent people of colour and 'those living with AIDS...and those who have been lost to the disease.'

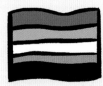

AROMANTIC

The most recent version of the aro flag was designed by Cameron (@cameronwhimsy) on Tumblr. The stripes symbolise the aromantic spectrum, platonic relationships and the different relationships that aro people might have to sexual attraction.

ASEXUAL

Unlike some of the other flags with solitary designers, the ace flag was created through online discussion and polling to create a design the existing community felt reflected them.

BISEXUAL

This flag was created by Michael Page in 1998. The design was inspired by an existing symbol of bisexuality known as the 'biangles' – two overlapping pink and dark blue triangles.

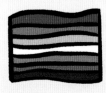

LESBIAN

There are several lesbian flag designs, but this is the one I use, which was created as recently as 2018. The design looks to be inclusive of trans lesbians, as well as lesbians across the spectrum of gender expression.

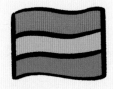

PANSEXUAL

Created online by Tumblr user Jasper around 2010, the pink represents people who are feminine, the blue represents masculine, while the yellow represents everything in between.

TRANS

This flag was created by Monica Helms in 1999, who said of the design: 'The light blue is the traditional colour for baby boys, pink is for girls and the white in the middle is for those who are transitioning, those who feel they have a neutral gender or no gender and those who are intersex.'

There are also other symbols and images that have specific ties to queer women.

VIOLETS

Originating in lesbian poet Sappho's verses – particularly an image of her and her lover wearing garlands of violets – this flower has become a symbol for queer women. In the 1920s, a play called *La Prisonnière* used violets as a lesbian symbol exchanged between two characters. Lesbians in Paris would reportedly wear the flower to show their support for the show.

DOUBLE VENUS SYMBOL

The double Venus symbol was also popularised in the 1970s. The symbol depicts two interlocking astronomical symbols for the planet Venus, a female gender symbol.

LABRYS

The labrys is a double-sided axe used by ancient civilisations, including as a symbol of the Amazons or feminine deities. In the 1970s, the symbol was adopted as a sign of strength and empowerment by feminist lesbian communities. It was then used by gay man Sean Campbell to create the original 'lesbian flag' in 1999.

This isn't an exhaustive list, and is based on the symbolism that exists where I am in the UK. Where you live, you might find other imagery that has a queer history. Plus, as our community continues to grow and develop, there may be new symbols, images and flags that emerge.

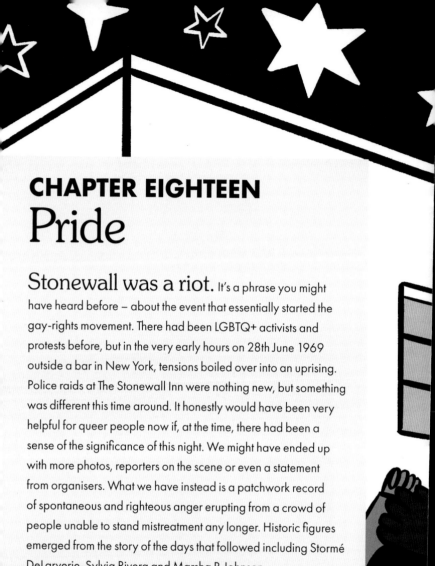

CHAPTER EIGHTEEN
Pride

Stonewall was a riot. It's a phrase you might have heard before – about the event that essentially started the gay-rights movement. There had been LGBTQ+ activists and protests before, but in the very early hours on 28th June 1969 outside a bar in New York, tensions boiled over into an uprising. Police raids at The Stonewall Inn were nothing new, but something was different this time around. It honestly would have been very helpful for queer people now if, at the time, there had been a sense of the significance of this night. We might have ended up with more photos, reporters on the scene or even a statement from organisers. What we have instead is a patchwork record of spontaneous and righteous anger erupting from a crowd of people unable to stand mistreatment any longer. Historic figures emerged from the story of the days that followed including Stormé DeLarverie, Sylvia Rivera and Marsha P. Johnson.

The riots lasted for days, spurred on by reports of the events in gay newspapers at the time, that brought new waves of protesters in support. The aftermath had long-lasting effects for our community, including the formation of multiple LGBTQ+ organisations around the world, and the creation of the annual Pride march and protest which began the following year in cities across the world. From there, more days of celebration were created – from visibility days to remembrance days – marking moments for our community to come together to honour our past and our present.

Pride might have started as a march, but today many cities hold events over weeks, or even an entire month, in addition to the main parade. If you live in (or can make it to) one of these areas you can expect things like:

• The main Pride parade
• Parties and evening events
• Educational talks
• Community workshops
• Volunteer opportunities

And you don't even have to spend time at these officially organised spaces – I've spent a few Prides in the sunshine in a park having a picnic with my queer friends. You don't have to know other LGBTQ+ people in real life to attend a Pride event – you can absolutely go on your own, and you might even make some queer friends while you're there! If you're nervous to go on your own, supportive allies (whether they are friends, family or partners) are always welcome at Pride too!

Pride is what you make of it. For some people, it involves drinking and dancing – a way to celebrate our community and how far we've come. For others it's about protest and activism, and looking forward to things we still have to fight for.

My experiences of Pride are usually a mix of the two.

I've been really lucky to live in London most of my life, a city that always has a big Pride parade and lots of events alongside it. But I know there's probably a lot of you reading this book right now who can't attend events openly, or maybe don't have any events near you. That doesn't mean you have to miss out on the Pride experience altogether.

• Check out online Pride events: there are often free digital panels, meet-ups and discussions over the summer months you can attend from anywhere in the world.

• Curate your own personal Pride Day at home: this might involve reading about queer history, watching queer movies, jamming to a playlist of gay artists, supporting LGBTQ+ charities by donating money or time to their efforts or decorating your house for the occasion!

• Spend time with supportive friends: just because you can't make it to a huge gathering doesn't mean you can't spend time with your own community (whether in person or online).

Maybe you don't have a Pride event happening near you, so you want to help set one up yourself. Go for it! I got involved in running Pride events at my uni and it was so much fun planning supportive and joyous spaces for other young queer people. You don't have to start planning a massive city-wide parade – in fact, that is definitely too much for one gal to handle! Think about small things, like running a social meet up for queer students in the local area at your school, or inviting an LGBTQ+ author you admire to a talk at your local library. Either would be a great start to begin building a small community for future events together.

CHAPTER NINETEEN
The Joy of Queerness

And so, we've reached the end of this book. We've taken a quick-stop tour through queer history, representation and experiences together over these pages, but I wanted to leave you with the most important chapter of all. Too many people and pressures in LGBTQ+ people's lives tell us the negative things about being who we are. They tell us about fear and suffering, isolation and loss. I don't ever want to deny the experiences of people in our community who go through those things. But I think it's so vital to talk about what a joyous and wonderful experience being queer is.

A Note on the Author

Selina Nwulu is a writer of Nigerian heritage. Her poetry and essays have been widely featured in a variety of journals, short films and anthologies, including the critically acclaimed anthology *New Daughters of Africa*. Her first chapbook collection, *The Secrets I Let Slip* was published in 2015 by Burning Eye Books and is a Poetry Book Society recommendation.

She has toured her poetry extensively, both internationally and throughout the UK in a number of cultural institutions. She has also been featured in *Vogue*, *ES* Magazine, *i-D* and *Blavity* amongst others. Her work has been translated into Spanish, Greek and Polish, and exhibited in Warsaw, New York, Dublin and Glasgow. She was Young Poet Laureate for London in 2015-6, an award that showcases literary talent across the capital and was shortlisted for the Brunel International African Poetry Prize 2019. She is also a finalist for the 2021 UK Arts Award for Environmental Writing. *A Little Resurrection* is her debut full-length collection.

A Note on the Type

Warnock is a serif typeface designed by Robert Slimbach. The design features sharp, wedgeshaped serifs. The typeface is named after John Warnock, one of the co-founders of Adobe. John Warnock's son, Chris Warnock, requested that Slimbach design the typeface as a tribute to his father in 1997. It was later released as a commercial font by Adobe in 2000 under the name Warnock Pro.

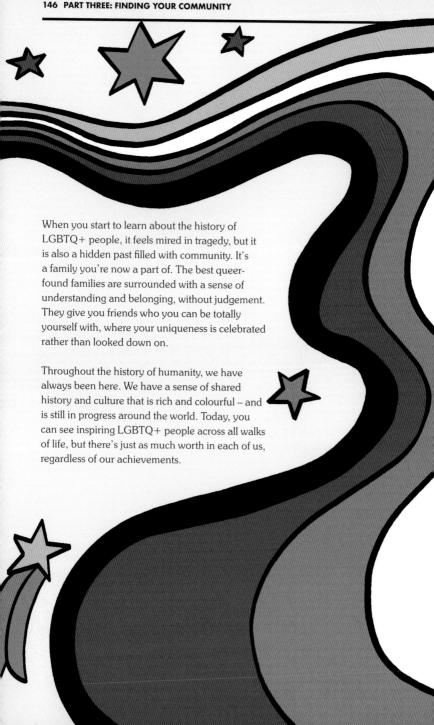

When you start to learn about the history of LGBTQ+ people, it feels mired in tragedy, but it is also a hidden past filled with community. It's a family you're now a part of. The best queer-found families are surrounded with a sense of understanding and belonging, without judgement. They give you friends who you can be totally yourself with, where your uniqueness is celebrated rather than looked down on.

Throughout the history of humanity, we have always been here. We have a sense of shared history and culture that is rich and colourful – and is still in progress around the world. Today, you can see inspiring LGBTQ+ people across all walks of life, but there's just as much worth in each of us, regardless of our achievements.

That first step of figuring out who you are might seem daunting and scary at first, but it is a journey of self-discovery that many people never get to go on. At the end of it, you have begun to truly know yourself – to question assumptions and ideas that society has placed on you, and come out the other side with a sense of inner authenticity. There is a strength in the resilience and vulnerability it takes to live your life openly and freely.

You have such a brilliant life ahead of you, full of queer joy – so go out there and live it.

THINKING POINTS

What are your feelings towards femininity or the notion of being perceived as feminine?

Are there examples of gender stereotypes that you notice in your everyday life?

What are your feelings about your gender, if any?

What are your feelings on masculinity or the notion of being perceived as masculine?

How much of a role do you think cisnormativity plays in the media?

Has compulsory heterosexuality affected your life? If so, how?

What are your feelings on androdgny or the notion of being perceived as androgynous?

Have you ever had something personal publicised or exposed before you were ready for everyone to find out? How did it make you feel?

Consider everything you have read in this book. How much of this do you remember learning at school?

What does safe space mean to you?

What does Pride mean to you?

GLOSSARY

Ableism – discrimination against disabled people.

Ace – short for asexual. Someone who experiences little or no sexual attraction to other people.

Activism – campaigning to bring about political or social change.

Ally – a person who uses their privilege to help the cause of a marginalised group, without themselves belonging to that group.

Ambulatory wheelchair user – a person who uses a wheelchair, but can walk in some circumstances.

Androgynous – presenting as a mix of qualities linked to masculinity and femininity – or being neither distinguishably masculine nor feminine.

Bigotry – being unreasonably prejudiced against a person or people, just because they belong to a certain group.

Biphobia – a feeling of hostility, disdain or prejudice against bisexual people.

Cis – short for cisgender. Describes a person whose gender identity matches the sex and gender they were assumed to be at birth.

Compulsory heterosexuality – the idea that heterosexuality is assumed and enforced upon people by a patriarchal and heteronormative society.

Consent – agreement given by two or more different parties.

Contraception – the use of a method, such as a condom or other techniques, to prevent pregnancy and STDs (sexually transmitted diseases).

Destigmatise – to take away negative associations from something once regarded as bad.

Fatphobia – a feeling of hostility, disdain or prejudice against fat people.

Fetish – when someone is interested in something sexually to a large degree.

Gender binary – the idea that people can be classified into one of just two distinct and opposite genders – male or female. The gender binary often supports the idea that people will align closely with socially constructed ideas of masculinity (if they're male) or femininity (if they're female). It is a very limited idea of gender and gender expression.

Gender expression – the way in which we present ourselves (including clothing, hairstyles and behaviour) which might be associated with how the world views gender. Your gender expression and gender identity don't have to 'match' – you might identify as a girl but enjoy presenting yourself in a way that society deems as 'masculine', for example.

Gender identity – our personal understanding and experience of our gender, and how we label our gender.

Gender non-conforming – relating to a person whose behaviour or appearance does not fit with cultural and social norms about what is expected of their gender.

Heteronormativity – the assumption across society that everyone is straight and that heterosexuality is the only 'correct' sexuality.

Internalised homophobia – negative thoughts and associations that LGBTQ+ people have about their sexuality. Similar feelings might be internalised biphobia or internalised transphobia, in bi and trans people, for example.

Intersectionality – a way of understanding how aspects of a person's social and political identities combine to create different experiences of discrimination and privilege. The term was conceptualised by Kimberlé Williams Crenshaw.

Masturbation – stimulation of your own genitals for sexual pleasure.

Obfuscation – the action of deliberately making something unclear or hard to understand.

OCD – short for Obsessive Compulsive Disorder, which is a mental health condition where people experience recurring intrusive thoughts and repetitive behaviours that they cannot control.

Ostracisation – to exclude a person from society or from a community by not communicating with them or by refusing to acknowledge their presence.

Outing – the act of disclosing a person's sexual orientation or gender identity without consent.

Prejudice – an opinion or belief about something that is not based on logic or actual experience.

Pride – an event celebrating the lesbian, gay, bisexual, transgender, non-binary and queer community.

Queer – a word that has been used as both a slur against the LGBTQ+ community and as a

reclaimed umbrella term for it. It is used as an identity label by individuals for a number of reasons including as a catch-all term when they have multiple queer identities (e.g. gay and asexual), or for people who feel like other more defined labels don't fit them.

Questioning – someone who is not sure or exploring how they identify in terms of their sexuality and/or gender identity.

Sapphic – an umbrella term that includes any woman who experiences any attraction to other women (including bi, lesbian, pan and queer women).

Sexual anatomy – the sex organs on the outside of your body, and the sex and reproductive organs on the inside of your body.

Sexual orientation/sexuality – a person's identity in relation to the gender or genders to which they are sexually attracted.

STDs – stands for Sexually Transmitted Diseases. These are infections that are passed on through sex or intimate contact with another person.

Stonewall riots – a series of spontaneous protests by the queer community in response to a police raid at the Stonewall Inn in New York City on June 28th 1969.

Trans – short for transgender. It's sometimes used specifically to refer to someone who transitions between binary genders of male and female, but can also be used as an umbrella term for anyone whose gender identity doesn't match the sex and gender that they were assumed to be at birth.

Transmisogyny – the combination of transphobia and misogyny towards trans women and transfeminine people that creates a form of oppression not fully shared by either cisgender women or trans men.

Transphobia – a feeling of hostility, disdain or prejudice against trans people.

UK Black Pride – is a Black gay pride event in London that has taken place since 2005. It's Europe's largest celebration for African, Asian, Middle Eastern, Latin American and Caribbean heritage LGBTQ+ people, attracting thousands of people annually. There are Black Pride organisations and events held in the US, too, such as Atlanta Black Pride and D.C. Black Pride.

TAKE IT FURTHER

· *This Book is Gay* by Juno Dawson

· *What's the T?* by Juno Dawson

· *Proud* by various authors and Juno Dawson

· *Stone Butch Blues* by Leslie Feinberg

· *Hood Feminism: Notes from the Women White Feminists Forgot* by Mikki Kendall

· *Sister Outsider* by Audre Lorde

· *Queerly Autistic: The Ultimate Guide For LGBTQIA+ Teens On The Spectrum Book* by Erin Ekins

· *Trans Teen Survival Guide* by Owl and Fox Fisher

· *The Times I Knew I Was Gay* by Eleanor Crewes

· *Ace* by Angela Chen

· *The New Queer Conscience* by Adam Eli

· *Queer: A Graphic History* by Meg-John Barker and Jules Scheele

· *Free to Be Me: An LGBTQ+ Journal of Love, Pride and Finding Your Inner Rainbow* by Dom&Ink

- *Sex Education* (2019)

- *I Am Jazz* (2015)

- *Pride* (2014)

- *Pose* (2018)

- *Boy Meets Girl* (2014)

- *The Miseducation of Cameron Post* (2018)

- *Nanette* (2017)

- *Blockers* (2018)

- *The Half of It* (2020)

Remember to check the age-range of these films and TV shows before watching.

SUPPORT

LGBT Switchboard – a dedicated helpline for LGBTQ+ people. They can talk through anything with you and nothing is off-limits.

switchboard.lgbt

0300 330 0630

Mermaids UK – provides familial and individual support for gender diverse and transgender children and young people.

mermaidsuk.org.uk

0808 801 0400

MindLine Trans+ – a confidential mental health support helpline for LGBTQ+ people.

mindlinetrans.org.uk

0300 330 5468

Stonewall Youth – contact them for helpful advice and information. If you need to talk to someone, you can also call the Stonewall information service.

www.stonewall.org.uk

0800 0502020

The Proud Trust – a charity that supports LGBTQ+ youth. They have lots of help and advice for young people on their website, and a free and confidential instant messaging service.

www.theproudtrust.org

Childline – a free counselling service for children and young people up to the age of 19. Their phone service is open 24 hours a day, 7 days a week, so there's always someone to talk to.

www.childline.org.uk

0800 1111

Samaritans – a free 24-hour helpline. You can talk about anything you want, without judgement, and there's always someone there to listen.

www.samaritans.org

116 123

Albert Kennedy Trust (akt) – supports LGBTQ+ people aged 16-25 who are homeless or living in difficult circumstances. They have an instant messaging service on their website.

www.akt.org.uk

Gender Identity Research & Education Society – works to improve the lives of trans and gender non-conforming people of all ages.

www.gires.org.uk

Terrence Higgins Trust – provides support for LGBTQ+ people worried about their sexual health, with a particular focus on people living with HIV.

www.tht.org.uk

0808 802 1221

Mind Out – information and mental health support specifically for LGBTQ+ people.

mindout.org.uk

ACKNOWLEDGEMENTS

Rowan

This is the part where I have to say some thank yous…

To my family for being so supportive of me, and my queer identity, since before I even came out. None of this would have been possible without you.

To Annie, Hafsa, Maz and Mikaela, for offering your thoughts, stories, and ideas to your sections of this book. I couldn't have asked for better contributors to this book, and I know there will be so many readers who needed to hear you.

To my agent Tamara Kawar. Your enthusiasm for this book and what it was trying to do has been a dream – and it doesn't hurt that we have the same taste in fanfic.

To Lucy Menzies and the whole team at Quarto for understanding so perfectly exactly what this book could be, and supporting me as a baby author to make it happen.

To Jacky Sheridan for making this book complete with your unbelievably joyful and relatable illustrations, I'm so glad we managed to find you.

To Nikki Thomas for taking an absolutely banging author photo for me with about 24-hours notice – it makes me feel very legit.

And finally, to all my queer friends, especially Bren, Ellen, Krish, Nikki, Ruby and Yaz for listening to all my chaotic voice memos while figuring out how to write this book – and for being your incredible authentic selves.

Jacky

I'd like to thank the maker of the Queercore playlist on Spotify, and my queer girl gang for acting as my sounding board for ideas in the group chat on a regular basis – Helen, Ciara & Kingzo.

Thanks to Diet Coke, and my partner Billy and housemate and illustrator pal Fiona for all the moral support throughout drawing this book.

Huge thanks as well to Karissa for all her patience and for her beautiful design work, and last but not least to Rowan for writing such an important and informative book that I could have really done with being in the world when I was a teenager.

Hafsa

I'd like to thank my spouse Nick for loving me because of who I am, not in spite of it.

Mikaela

I want to thank Rowan for making all of this happen, and for reaching out and asking if I'd like to be part of this wonderful project, as well as her patience with my initial drafts; Lucy, for being a fantastic liaison (and also very patient); my fellow contributors, alongside whom I feel very humbled to included; the folks who shared the real life of my story with me – Annie, Paige and Sarah – so that I could share the retelling with you; and most especially, my girlfriend Sarah, without whom I wouldn't have the tale to tell, nor the self-assurance to know it was worth telling.

And to every queer, trans, disfigured and disabled person: thank you for living. Living is enough. You are enough.

Annie

To my chosen family and communities, your existence is magnificent!

Inspiring | Educating | Creating | Entertaining

Brimming with creative inspiration, how-to projects, and useful information to enrich your everyday life, The Quarto Group is a favourite destination for those pursuing their interests and passions. Visit our site and dig deeper with our books into your area of interest: Quarto Creates, Quarto Cooks, Quarto Homes, Quarto Lives, Quarto Drives, Quarto Explores, Quarto Gifts, or Quarto Kids.

First Published in 2022 by Frances Lincoln Children's Books, an imprint of The Quarto Group.
The Old Brewery, 6 Blundell Street, London N7 9BH, United Kingdom.
T (0)20 7700 6700 F (0)20 7700 8066 **www.Quarto.com**

The illustrations were created digitally
Set in Futura and ITC Souvenir

Published by Peter Marley
Designed by Karissa Santos
Commissioned and edited by Lucy Menzies
With editorial assistance from Rachel Robinson
Production by Dawn Cameron

With thanks to Tora Brumalis and Matt Smith

Manufactured in Singapore, CO012022

9 8 7 6 5 4 3 2 1

MIX
Paper from
responsible sources
FSC™ C007207
www.fsc.org

THE 2022 BLOOMSBURY POETRY SERIES

April
Music for the Dead and Resurrected
by Valzhyna Mort

Music for the Dead and Resurrected captures the complexity of living in the shadows of imperial force, of the vulnerability of bodies, of seeing with more than one's eyes.

Valzhyna Mort's work is characterised by a memorial sensibility that honours those lost to the violences of nation states. In *Music for the Dead and Resurrected* the poet offers us a body of work which balances political import with serious play. There are few poets writing with such an intuitive sense of the balance between arcane and contemporary currents in poetry. Mort's lines are timeless, finely honed to last beyond a single lifetime.

June
Sonnets for Albert by Anthony Joseph

With *Sonnets for Albert*, Anthony Joseph returns to the autobiographical material explored in his earlier collection *Bird Head Son*. In this followup he weighs the impact of being the son of an absent, or mostly absent father, in poems that, though they threaten to break under the weight of their emotions, are always masterfully poised as the stylish man they depict.

October
A Little Resurrection by Selina Nwulu

A Little Resurrection, the debut full-length collection of Selina Nwulu, is the work of a questing sensibility. These poems are equally at home in the golden light of Senegal as they are in the harsh winds of Yorkshire. In these poems blackness itself is complicated, extending the resonances of being to reflect the self in a state of flux, a fugitive spirit battling the harm of erasure. There is a profound joy in these poems, all the more powerful for being hard-won. This book heralds the branching out of an important trajectory in Anglophone poetry.

November
The Lost Chronicle: 2004–2009 by Polarbear

Polarbear is one of the most influential poets of his generation. The work collected here is the work that made his name. These poems have racked up hundreds of thousands of views online, lodging themselves in the hearts and minds of readers and audiences alike. His particular gift is for the many kinds of music a line can contain. He marries the intricate, compulsive, rhyming strategies of rap with the schanachie's gift for telling a story and the saxophonist's flair for bending the possibilities of sound.